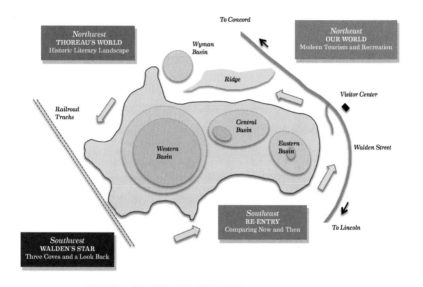

Map of Walden Pond showing the path of our counterclockwise tour. Beginning at the Visitor Center (right), we will travel through four different sectors, each with its own theme. The edges and deep portions of the lake's four kettle basins are shown schematically, along with several other features. North is up.

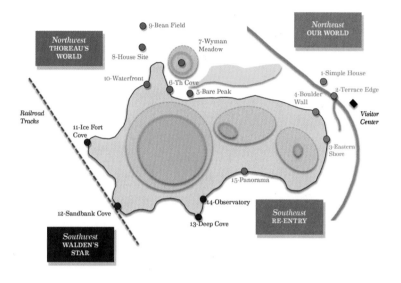

Map of Walden Pond showing the number, name, and location of each of our fifteen stops. The stops are color-coded by sector and theme. To locate stops on the park's official Trail Map or on the modern topography, consult the two maps on the back endpapers of this guide. North is up.

# The Guide
## to Walden Pond

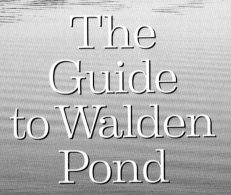

# The
# Guide
# to Walden
# Pond

## Robert M. Thorson

An
Exploration of
the History,
Nature,
Landscape,
and
Literature
of One of
America's Most
Iconic Places

HOUGHTON MIFFLIN HARCOURT
BOSTON    NEW YORK · 2018

For information about permission to reproduce selections from this book,
write to Permissions, Houghton Mifflin Harcourt Publishing Company,
3 Park Avenue, 19th Floor, New York, New York 10016.

hmco.com

*Library of Congress Cataloging-in-Publication Data*
Names: Thorson, Robert M., 1951- author.
Title: The guide to Walden Pond : an exploration of the history, nature, landscape,
and literature of one of America's most iconic places / Robert M. Thorson.
Description: Boston : Houghton Mifflin Harcourt, 2018. | Includes bibliographical
references and index.
Identifiers: LCCN 2017054034 (print) | LCCN 2017052209 (ebook) |
ISBN 9781328969842 (ebook) | ISBN 9781328969217 (paperback) |
ISBN 9781328489173 (paper over board)
Subjects: LCSH: Walden Pond (Middlesex County, Mass.) — History — Guidebooks. |
Thoreau, Henry David, 1817-1862 — Homes and haunts — Massachusetts —
Walden Woods — Guidebooks. | Authors, American — Homes and haunts —
Massachusetts — Middlesex County — Guidebooks. | BISAC: NATURE /
Ecosystems & Habitats / Lakes, Ponds & Swamps. | HISTORY / United States /
State & Local / New England (CT, MA, ME, NH, RI, VT). | SPORTS & RECREATION /
Hiking.
Classification: LCC F72.M7 (print) | LCC F72.M7 T54 2018 (ebook) |
DDC 974.4/4 — dc23
LC record available at https://lccn.loc.gov/2017054034

Book design by Eugenie S. Delaney
Printed in China
SCP 10 9 8 7 6 5 4 3 2 1

To enthusiasts of Walden and *Walden*

# CONTENTS

Timelines    viii

Preface    1

**PREPARATION**    7

Fame    7

Preview    15

People    23

Questions    25

Using This Guide    26

**THE TOUR**    31

**Northeast:**
**Our World**    33

1. Simple House    35

2. Terrace Edge    47

3. Eastern Shore    61

4. Boulder Wall    73

**Northwest:**
**Thoreau's World**    83

5. Bare Peak    87

6. Thoreau's Cove    95

7. Wyman Meadow    105

8. House Site    117

9. Bean Field    137

10. Waterfront    145

**Southwest:**
**Walden's Star**    156

11. Ice Fort Cove    159

12. Sandbank Cove    171

13. Deep Cove    179

14. Observatory    189

**Southeast:**
**Re-entry**    199

15. Panorama    201

**LOOKING BACK**    213

Acknowledgments    217

Notes    219

Organizations    233

Further Readings    237

Index    241

# TIMELINES

## *Walden,* the Author

*A native son of Concord, Henry David Thoreau (1817–1862) spends most of his life living with his family on an American Main Street. Though writing is his chosen vocation, he supports himself as a day laborer, pencil manufacturer, teacher, and land surveyor.*

**1817**    Born on July 12 to Cynthia (Dunbar) Thoreau (1787–1872) and John Thoreau (1787–1859) and baptized David Henry in First Parish Unitarian Church. Siblings include Helen (1812–1849), John (1815–1842), and Sophia (1819–1876).

**1822**    Sees Walden Pond for the first time, probably from the Terrace Edge.

**1824**    Visits Walden Pond with his family from what would later be called Thoreau's Cove.

**1833**    Attends Harvard College after narrowly passing entrance exams. His study emphasizes language, literature, history, and philosophy.

**1837**    Reads Ralph Waldo Emerson's *Nature.* Graduates from college. Changes name to Henry David. Lives in shanty at Flint's Pond for six weeks with college friend Stearns Wheeler. Begins and quits teaching at Concord Academy. Meets and befriends Emerson. Begins his life work, the *Journal.*

**1839**    Takes boat trip up Merrimack River with brother John. Proposes marriage to Ellen Sewall and is rejected, thereafter becoming a "bachelor of thought and Nature."

**1840**    Befriends Amos Bronson Alcott and his family, especially the daughters Louisa May and Abigail May.

**1841**    Lives and works at Emerson's house from April 1841 to May 1843. Expresses in writing a desire to live near a pond, probably either Flint's Pond or Fairhaven Pond.

**1842** Brother and best friend John dies of lockjaw, a turning point in Thoreau's life. Befriends William Ellery Channing, his most frequent sojourning companion.

**1845** Builds a wooden house at Walden Pond and plants the Bean Field. Moves from the family's "Texas House" in Concord to Walden Pond on July 4.

**1847** Lectures in Lincoln and Concord about his life at Walden Pond. His lecture, "A History of Myself," becomes *Walden*'s first draft. Leaves Walden Pond on September 6 to live in the Emersons' house at the invitation of Lidian Emerson.

**1849** Self-publishes *A Week on the Concord and Merrimack Rivers* in May. Its commercial failure forces him to abandon his *Walden* project and become a land surveyor.

**1850** Thoreau family moves from the Texas House to the large "Yellow House" at 255 Main Street, where Henry lives until his death twelve years later.

**1851** Reads Charles Darwin's *Voyage of the Beagle*. Deeply inspired, he becomes a self-taught scientific naturalist and returns to the *Walden* manuscript with a new focus on nature. Visits Walden Pond regularly to make observations. Drafts four, five, and six follow.

**1854** Writes final, seventh draft of *Walden* in late winter. Submits manuscript in mid-March. Published on August 9 as *Walden; or, Life in the Woods*.

**1862** Dies of consumption (tuberculosis) on May 6. Public funeral held in First Parish Unitarian Church on May 9.

## *Walden*, the Book

*Thoreau's masterpiece about living deliberately at Walden Pond is published in Boston on August 9, 1854, by Ticknor and Fields. The final book manuscript results from seven handwritten drafts from two great bursts of writing over a period of nine years.*

**1854** Ticknor and Fields of Boston publishes *Walden; or, Life in the Woods* on August 9. Reviews are generally favorable, but mixed. The first printing of 2000 copies takes more than five years to sell out.

**1862** A limited edition of *Walden* is brought back into print by James Fields shortly after Thoreau's death. The title is shortened to *Walden*. Published eulogies and posthumous publication of Thoreau's works raise his profile as an author.

**1882** Houghton Mifflin (successor of Ticknor and Fields) publishes Franklin Sanborn's *Henry D. Thoreau* in its prestigious *American Men of Letters* series. This third biography solidifies Thoreau's reputation.

**1893** The Riverside edition of Thoreau's works (six volumes including *Walden*) is published by Houghton Mifflin.

**1906** Thoreau's *Journal* is published in fourteen volumes by Houghton Mifflin, broadening Thoreau's appeal, and putting *Walden* in a biographic perspective.

**1936** *Walden* enters the American literary canon via publication of *The Flowering of New England 1815–1865* by historian Van Wyck Brooks.

**1941** Founding of the Thoreau Society. *Walden* exists in ninety-eight editions.

**2017** Bicentennial of Thoreau's birth is celebrated internationally. *Walden* exists in more than a thousand editions.

## Walden, the Place

*Thoreau's world-famous residency at the pond (1845–1847) is only one of many historical events responsible for creating the place we know today. Nearly as important were the arrival of the railroad (1844) and automobiles (1902) and donation of land for the park (1922).*

**before 1635**  Archaeological negative evidence indicates that isolated Walden Pond is little visited by indigenous peoples whose settlements are located along the nearby rivers where the resources are richer.

**1635**  Concord is chartered as an English Puritan plantation on the Concord River about one and a quarter miles north of what would later be called Walden Pond.

**1653**  Walden Pond is mapped by English colonists in a remote woodland.

**1754**  Lincoln is created as a separate town from Concord. The road between these colonial villages passes by the pond.

**1795**  Cato Ingraham, a freed slave, moves to a house northeast of Walden Pond. His dwelling is one of several in a community living in poverty at the edge of town in the late eighteenth century.

**1836**  Ralph Waldo Emerson highlights the beauty of ponds in his famous essay *Nature*. Walden Pond becomes the center of the transcendental "lake district," modeled after the English Lake District of the romantic poets.

**1843**  Construction of the Fitchburg Railroad industrializes the western side of Walden Pond and partially fills one of its coves with earthen debris. Hundreds of Irish laborers and their families live near the pond. Railroad opens in June 1844.

**1845** Thoreau builds a house at Walden Pond, moves in on July 4, and stays three summers and two winters until September 6, 1847.

**1847** Thoreau's house is hauled away up to Concord Street, leaving a cellar hole.

**1854** Walden becomes known beyond the local vicinity when *Walden* is published on August 9. The first literary pilgrims arrive to experience the sense of place.

**1861** Thoreau makes a last visit with sister Sophia in September.

**1866** Walden Lake Grove Excursion Park (aka Lake Walden amusement park) opens up near the railroad tracks at Ice Fort Cove and runs continuously until 1902.

**1885** Lake Walden is enshrined as a tourist destination in George B. Bartlett's *The Concord Guide Book: Historic, Literary, and Picturesque.*

**1902** Closure of the Lake Walden amusement park on Walden's western shore coincides with the arrival of the first automobiles above the Eastern Shore. Autos will eventually bring untold millions of visitors to the lake.

**1922** Walden Pond State Reservation is created after donation of 80 acres of land by Concord families. The park is rapidly developed.

**1931** The Pond Path is cut around the perimeter, broadening access and initiating a wave of erosion and bank collapse. Finished in 1935.

**1957** The "Save Walden Committee," led by Gladys Hosmer, Ruth Wheeler, and Edwin Way Teale, is created to fight plans for massive construction along the Eastern Shore.

**1962** Walden Pond becomes a National Historic Landmark. Passage of the U.S. Wilderness Act of 1964 underscores *Walden* as a cornerstone of the environmental movement.

**1974** The newly created state Department of Environmental Management assumes responsibilities for preserving Walden Pond and limits attendance to 1,000 people.

**1990** The nonprofit Walden Woods Project is created as the successor to a variety of local environmental/conservation organizations. Its Thoreau Institute opens in 1998.

**2003** The newly created state Department of Conservation and Recreation assumes management responsibilities as part of its state park system.

**2004** W. Barksdale Maynard publishes *Walden Pond: A History*.

**2017** The new Visitor Center, complete with exhibits and a film, opens to celebrate the bicentennial of Thoreau's birth. This guide quickly follows.

## Walden, the Landform

*Walden Pond is created when groundwater fills a slowly deepening void being made by the underground melting of buried glacial ice. The ice has been trapped in a bedrock valley and is later filled with sand and gravel during retreat of the last ice sheet. Dates are approximate.*

**350,000,000 years ago** The bedrock beneath Walden Pond (Andover Granite) is created when molten rock with a pudding-like consistency squeezes up from below and freezes in place. This occurs when ancestral North America collides with a ribbon-shaped continent called Avalonia.

**260,000,000 years ago** The final continental collision responsible for creating New England ends. Fracturing and faulting of the Andover Granite during the collision has created a zone of weakness that later allows the erosion of a bedrock valley beneath what is now Concord's "chain of ponds."

**25,000 years ago**   The last of four ice sheets covers Concord as it flows toward Martha's Vineyard. This stream of slowly moving solid ice several thousand feet thick deepens the ancient bedrock valley to create a depression where Walden Pond is today.

**16,000 years ago**   As the climate warms, the great ice sheet thins and its edge migrates northward to reach present-day Concord. Masses of stagnant ice left in the bottom of the bedrock valley are buried by sand and gravel. A potent meltwater river creates a vast, flat delta plain of braided channels flowing toward the southwest.

**14,000 years ago**   Final melting of deeply buried ice leaves colossal "sinkhole" depressions below the formerly flat delta plain. These depressions, or basins, are known to geologists as kettles. Walden Pond and others in a local "chain of ponds" are created when these kettles sink below the water table. By this time, the delta plain and adjacent slopes have become vegetated with tundra, which transitions into forest.

**1843 C.E.**  Construction of the Fitchburg Railroad requires the filling of a western cove with earthen debris to create what Thoreau calls the "railroad sandbank." This is the first significant change to the pond since glaciation.

**1957 C.E.**  A century of construction transforms the Eastern Shore into a recreational swimming facility capable of handling thousands of swimmers per day. Prior to this makeover, there is only a short, thin, pebbly beach. Human impacts continue.

# PREFACE

My first trip around Walden Pond was on a hot summer day in 1985. For me it was a personal pilgrimage to Henry David Thoreau's original House Site, where I dropped a smooth granite pebble from Alaska. For my wife and toddlers, it was a happy family adventure. I recall a crowded sandy beach, a trout fisherman in a kayak, a young woman reading in woodsy shade, and the astonishing clarity of Walden's turquoise water.

Since that first trip, I've been guiding all sorts of groups around Walden Pond: students, friends, relatives, church groups, park naturalists, and participants in national conferences and workshops. My take-home message has been the same for everyone. This 62-acre lake wasn't the *backdrop* for Thoreau's famous experiment in deliberate living. It was the *centerpiece* of his experience, a body of water that defined and shaped Thoreau's masterpiece, *Walden*. In short, the *place of his book* gave rise to the *book of his place,* which spawned America's environmental consciousness.

As the 2017 bicentennial celebration of Thoreau's birthday approached, I began a conversation with the staff of the Walden Woods Project (WWP) about developing a guide based on the tours I've been leading. The WWP is a nonprofit organization devoted to the "land, literature, and legacy of Henry David Thoreau to foster an ethic of environmental stewardship and social responsibility." This book is the result of that conversation, conceived as a copiously illustrated guide to the *outdoor* experience at Walden Pond to

complement the *indoor* experience of the park's Visitor Center. By "park," I mean Walden Pond State Reservation, a 335-acre parcel managed within the state park system by the Massachusetts Department of Conservation and Recreation (DCR). By "Visitor Center," I mean the beautiful 2016 wooden building, now with introductory exhibits, video theater, bookshop, and other facilities.

*The Guide to Walden Pond* is a hybrid mix of four well-known genres: travel guide, nature guide, trail guide, and travel literature. This book is part travel guide, having maps and essential information. It's part nature guide because Thoreau's favorite animals and plants are systematically described and placed in their natural habitats. It's part trail guide because trail directions and landscape descriptions are provided. It's part travel literature because the text is anecdotal and the content changes with each place. As a hybrid, this guide allows readers to pursue their own mix of interests.

I invite you to join me in exploring one of America's most iconic places. Together, we will emulate Thoreau's walking style, which he

called "sauntering"—connoting pilgrimage—and "sojourning"—connoting a temporary remove from normal life. With great expectations, he stepped out into nature until something caught his attention. He paused to explore that something, reflected on its meaning, and then moved on to the next something. For the New England transcendentalists, this sort of slow journey was called an *amble*. Their predecessors, the romantic poets of the English Lake District, called it walking in the *peripatetic* style. The term originates with Aristotle, who created a school of philosophy based on this method of walking, pausing, learning, and enjoying.

This oblique aerial view of Walden Pond looks north into Thoreau's Cove. Our tour will be counterclockwise around the pond from the Visitor Center at far right. (© Scot Miller)

Our counterclockwise tour around Walden Pond can be taken from anywhere in the world. All we need is a comfortable place to read and a willingness to let our imaginations guide us along. Our

The wide, shallow beach at Walden Pond was created during the twentieth century to accommodate heavy use by swimmers.

narrated journey will carry us around a body of water Thoreau called "earth's eye." Each of our fifteen stops has its own illustrated text. Four colored maps help guide us from one place to another, keep track of park trails, and show high-resolution topography. Four timelines provide quick historical reference. Seventy-five sidebars, fifteen "At a Glance" summaries, and a helpful list of resources will enrich our immersion into history, nature, landscape, and literature.

Alternatively, some of us will travel in person to Walden Pond to this street address: 915 Walden Street, Concord, Massachusetts. With boots on the ground and this guide in hand, we'll explore what Thoreau called a "gem of the woods." We'll be staying near the "Pond Path," the official, alliterative name for Walden's perimeter trail. It's an easy walk that curves gently left and right, and rises and falls without being steep. I offer step-by-step directions based on local landmarks and give the exact GPS (Global Positioning System) coordinates for each stop.

The ubiquity of handheld digital technology offers a third possibility. Using a favorite mobile device, we can explore what Thoreau called "God's Drop" in *virtual*, rather than *physical* space. Using free software applications, such as the geobrowser Google Earth, we can access satellite imagery to fly around the pond and hover over each stop as if in a helicopter or aerial drone.

Finally, there's a fourth option for taking the tour: using your memories to guide you along. Walden Pond has been a wildly popular tourist destination for more than a century. During recent decades, official visitation has been more than half a million people per year. People come for a variety of reasons: a summer swim, a literary pilgrimage, a walk in the woods, a school field trip, a bird-watching outing, or a bus tour. If you have memories of a previous trip to Walden Pond, this guide can help leverage them into an enhanced *sense of place.*

I wrote this guide to be user-friendly, keeping all four of these groups in mind: armchair readers, trail walkers, virtual tourists, and previous visitors. This allows each reader to individualize his or her own Walden experience.

Shall we begin?

Our tour begins and ends on the wooden ramp of the Visitor Center.

# PREPARATION

Walking through the tall glass doors of the Visitor Center, we move out onto the large wooden deck and into the fresh air. Keeping to the left, we descend the long, gentle ramp until our shoes crunch the stone dust on the ground-level path. The first of our fifteen stops lies directly ahead.

Where are we going? What will we see? Who will we meet? Why does it matter?

This introduction answers those questions. Reading it will be like the preparation you might make for any trip.

The first part of our preparation, "Fame," explains why this beautiful, but ordinary, body of water is world famous. "Preview" takes us on a whirlwind, round-trip journey through the pond's four geographic sectors, each with its own theme. "People" introduces readers to the cast of characters who played a role in the drama of Walden Pond before, during, and after Thoreau's two-year stay. "Questions" are those that rise to the top of the agenda for the park's interpretive program. "Using this Guide" explains the nuts and bolts of how this book is organized.

## Fame

Thoreau's *Walden; or, Life in the Woods* was published to mixed reviews in August 1854. The following year, summer resident Frank Bellew described Walden Pond as an "extinct gravel-pit, filled with the most exquisitely pure water." His plainspoken words convey a

The title page of *Walden; or, Life in the Woods* (1854) contains an engraving of Thoreau's house based on a sketch by his sister Sophia Thoreau. This highly stylized image shows the terrain and trees incorrectly. (Courtesy of the Walden Woods Project)

certain truth: Walden is indeed a gravel-rimmed hollow full of clean water, part of which has been excavated for gravel. Thoreau also downplayed his readers' expectations of the lake's beauty: "The scenery of Walden is on a humble scale, and, though very beautiful, does not approach to grandeur."

Indeed, Walden Pond will never be short-listed as a scenic Wonder of the World. During our tour, we won't be tramping through ancient groves of breathtaking sequoias; our woods will be unpretentious midsized oaks and pines. They sprouted after the great deforestation of Thoreau's era when wood—not coal, petroleum, or gas—was the primary fuel for the fireplaces and woodstoves of Concord, a bustling nineteenth-century market-and-manufacturing town surrounded by farms.

Humble Walden is a perfectly unassuming body of water, hereafter called both a lake and a pond. It's one of 50,000 comparable kettle lakes and ponds that speckle the northern United States in a sandy band between Nantucket Island, Massachusetts, and Great Falls, Montana. The state of Minnesota alone claims 10,000 lakes, many similarly created. Yet Walden Pond is singularly world famous. Why?

The short answer is that this *ordinary* place inspired an *extraordinary* book. For many, *Walden* is America's greatest work of literary nonfiction. Based on surveys done by the Modern Language Association, it's been the most widely studied. Hundreds of translated editions have permeated every corner of the globe. Thousands of writers and thinkers credit Thoreau's work as an inspiration. A very short list includes Walt Whitman, John Muir, John Burroughs, Frederick Law Olmsted, Leo Tolstoy, Sinclair Lewis, Herbert Wendell Gleason, Aldo Leopold, Robert Frost, Mohandas Gandhi, E. B. White, Joseph Wood Krutch, Rachel Carson, Loren Eiseley, Edwin Way Teale, Roger Tory Peterson, Edward Abbey, Martin Luther King Jr., Robert Pirsig, John F. Kennedy, Annie Dillard, Howard Zinn, Cesar Chavez, Garrison Keillor, Terry Tempest Williams, E. O. Wilson, Leslie Marmon Silko, Ann Zwinger, Alice Walker, Michael Pollan, Barbara Kingsolver, Rebecca Solnit, and Bill McKibben.

Before *Walden*'s 1854 publication, Walden Pond was known mainly to locals. Prior to Thoreau's 1862 death, "his beans sold better than his books," wrote Edward Abbey. Early posthumous publication of *The Maine Woods, Cape Cod, Excursions,* "Walking," and "Autumnal Tints" began to enhance his reputation. As early as 1872, readers were making literary pilgrimages to Walden Pond, pausing to add a stone to Thoreau's memorial cairn. By 1885, George B. Bartlett's *The Concord Guide Book* listed Walden Pond as a popular tourist attraction. During the 1890s, Thoreau's growing reputation was enhanced when Houghton Mifflin, the successor to *Walden*'s publisher Ticknor and Fields, published the Riverside edition of his collected works. In 1922 the pond and adjacent land were set aside as a state park, dubbed a "reservation." In 1936 and 1941, literary historians Van Wyck Brooks and F. O. Mathiessen canonized Thoreau within the pantheon of American authors, largely for *Walden*. In 1962, *Walden* the book helped inspire Rachel Carson's pathbreaking *Silent Spring*, and Walden the pond was designated a National Historic Landmark. Thoreau's famous line "In Wildness is the preservation of the world" helped ensure passage of the Wilderness Act of 1964, forever enshrining Walden Pond as the fountainhead of America's environmental movement.

The fame of Walden Pond depends utterly on the fame of Thoreau's masterpiece. This raises the question: What made his book so famous? It certainly helped that Henry was a social iconoclast and literary genius, and someone whose early death accelerated his reputation. It also helped that his posthumous legacy was skillfully promoted by a devoted group of friends and family, and by a few grateful readers. But similar circumstances are equally true for other authors.

What makes *Walden* special? Why did it rise to the top of the heap? Why did it achieve "hyper-canonical status as a cultural icon"? Why do some philosophers deem it "scripture"? I suggest four related answers: landscape, nature, solitude, and writing.

I begin with landscape. After watching the "morning star" rise over Walden Pond for two years, two months, and two days, Henry developed a hyper-concentrated sense of place. Effectively, he became *one* with nature, or as close to full immersion as most of us will ever get. He achieved this by self-identifying with the lake's solitude, purity, simplicity, sensitivity, strength, and renewal. These physical attributes of an actual place corresponded to the spiritual attributes he was seeking within himself as a human being. On our tour together, we will examine these same attributes at different places.

For example, when Thoreau declared "I am its stony shore," he was identifying with the tough simplicity of the wave-washed cobbles that encircled the pond in his day. When he wrote "I am no more lonely than the loon in the pond that laughs so loud," he was identifying with the solitary preferences of a magnificent bird. When he looked into the transparent water and asked "Walden, is that you?" he was seeing a reflection of his innermost thoughts.

Henry David Thoreau (1817–1862). A plaster cast of a marble bust by Walton Ricketson (1898). (Cast exhibited at the Walden Woods Thoreau Institute Library, courtesy of the Thoreau Society. The original bust is courtesy of the Concord Free Public Library.)

My second answer to why *Walden* is famous concerns organic nature. Thoreau wrote of his kinship with the living things that surrounded him. He felt the spirits of the trees and enjoyed the companionship of animal friends. Frederick Willis witnessed this in July 1847, after being brought to Thoreau's house by Bronson Alcott and his young daughters.

[Thoreau] was talking to Mr. Alcott of the wild flowers in Walden woods when, suddenly stopping, he said: 'Keep very still and I will show you my family.' Stepping quickly outside the cabin door, he gave a low and curious whistle; immediately a woodchuck came running towards him from a nearby burrow. With varying note, yet still low and strange, a pair of gray squirrels were summoned and approached him fearlessly. With still another note, several birds, including two crows, flew towards him, one of the crows nesting upon his shoulder . . . He fed them all from his hand, taking food from his pocket, and petted them gently before our delighted gaze; and then dismissed them by different whistling, always strange and low and short, each little wild thing departing instantly at hearing its special signal.

This book introduces fifteen members of Thoreau's animal family, one for each stop of our journey. Quotes from *Walden* link each creature to a specific place. Ditto for fifteen quotes about trees and shrubs that Thoreau loved, for fifteen sounds that resonated with him in respective places, and for fifteen insightful descriptions he wrote about the landscapes at our stops. These sixty lyrical passages show why Thoreau's *Walden* helped jump-start American nature writing as a distinct genre.

My third answer to *Walden*'s fame concerns solitude. Each of us needs just the right amount of quiet time. We need enough solitude to know ourselves as individuals, but not so much that we feel lonely. Thoreau found the right balance by living just inside the edge of the woods on the side of Walden Pond nearest the village. Each dawn found him deliciously alone, watching the sun rise over the water and feeling the pulse of nature beat within his heart. Each afternoon found him free to walk the railroad tracks to town so that he could experience the emotional warmth of a family home and engage

with the bustle of Main Street life. Each evening he had the option to join his friends and colleagues, often in Emerson's library. Thoreau was never the hermit, recluse, crank, or misfit

The red fox (*Vulpes vulpes*) was one of Thoreau's favorite animals for its mythological possibilities. See Stop 12, Sandbank Cove. (© Stefan Huwiler/image broker/Corbis)

that mythmakers want him to be. Instead, he was a gregarious, idiosyncratic genius on a personal mission to discover how a human life could be lived to the fullest.

In fact, Henry's remove to Walden Pond made him a local celebrity. He had more visitors at his house in the woods than when he lived in Concord village. When away from his house to sojourn in his rural landscape, he sought the companionship of woodchoppers, fishermen, farmers, and laborers. When hoeing his beans south of Walden Road, he hailed passersby with a wave, and they waved back. When he was moved to political action, Henry's house became a stop on the Underground Railroad for fugitive slaves. The fifteen

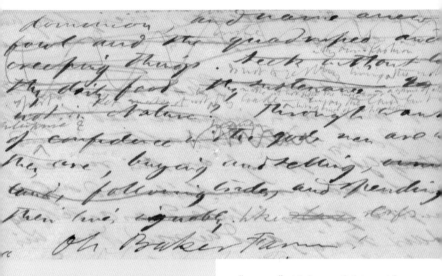

This detail of a leaf from the original *Walden* manuscript shows heavy editing in pencil on an inked text. Bottom line says "Oh Baker Farm!" (Courtesy of the Walden Woods Project)

"person" sidebars of this guide will introduce you to several of his close friends and to others who later shaped the history of Walden Pond for better or worse.

My fourth and most important answer to why *Walden* is famous involves the writing. Thoreau communicated his unique philosophy of human renewal in nature more effectively than anyone before or since. "Certainly no American," wrote Joyce Carol Oates, "has ever written more beautiful, vigorous, supple prose." Poet Robert Frost wrote that "in one book . . . he surpasses everything we have had in America."

Thoreau's literary accomplishment was the result of natural talent combined with extremely hard work and excellent training. There are seven known drafts of *Walden.* All were written longhand with an inkwell-dipped quill pen on paper over a period of nine years. Henry's editing marks were made with pencils he manufactured himself; his edits are dense and ubiquitous on all but the last draft. His literary colleagues—Ralph Waldo Emerson, his sister Sophia, Nathaniel Hawthorne, Margaret Fuller, Bronson Alcott, and William Ellery Channing—helped edit his work. His Harvard education concentrated on language and literature, notably ancient Greek, Latin, Hindi, and Norse, and contemporary French, Italian, and German. His professors included Cornelius Conway Felton, America's most influential classical scholar; Edward Tyrrel Channing, an endowed professor of rhetoric; and Henry Wadsworth Longfellow, America's most popular nineteenth-century poet. For Thoreau, the Harvard library was the best part of campus life. His intense engagement with hundreds of texts in multiple languages primed his pen, which flowed for seventeen postgraduate years before he sent his *Walden* masterpiece to the printer.

Thoreau's fusion of physical landscape, organic nature, sufficient solitude, and prose-poetry transformed an ordinary pond into a powerful symbol for his personal philosophy. "I am thankful that this pond was made deep and pure for a symbol," he concluded. His "lake of light" became holy water, within which he baptized himself anew every summer morning. Throughout our tour, we'll be linking the *book of his place* with the *place of his book*.

## Preview

Our journey will begin and end at the Visitor Center. Our walk in the woods will cover less than two miles on a tour that could easily take place on a single theoretical afternoon. We'll circumnavigate the pond following the Pond Path, a trodden trail of leaf litter, pine needles, twigs, acorns, humus, pebbles, dust, and rust. The dull palette of our path will surround a vivid lake whose colors Thoreau variously described as "misty bluish-green . . . vitreous greenish-blue . . . cerulean . . . glaucous . . . gray . . . silvery . . . black . . . azure . . .

The Pond Path was cut in the 1930s. Compaction from heavy foot traffic led to surface runoff and erosion, which continues today.

transparent." For us, the colors of the lake will vary with every angle, time of day, and type of weather.

The Visitor Center is located on a high gravel terrace above the Eastern Shore of Walden Pond. Though built of wood and designed to blend in with the trees, the Visitor Center is an ultramodern place. Behind the building are sun-tracking solar panels and automated parking kiosks. In front are flashing crosswalk signs and electronic buzzers. Below the terrace at lake level is a twentieth-century-engineered beach in constant need of twenty-first-century maintenance. The theme of this northeast sector of the park is "Our World" of modernity.

In this sector we will explore four stops in sequence. Simple House is one of dozens of twentieth-century replicas of Thoreau's original nineteenth-century house. At Terrace Edge we'll overlook the sharp brink between the ancient river terrace behind us and the colossal sinkhole (glacial kettle) holding Walden Pond. The lake's Eastern Shore was designed and built by architects and contractors working for the Middlesex County Commissioners. The engineered hardscape of cement and stone at Boulder Wall provides a chance to reflect on Thoreau's search for ultimate reality, and to explore Walden's deep prehistory.

This northeast sector of the pond was a trivial part of Thoreau's experience. It was invisible to him from where he lived: Henry's house was tucked behind a ridge and hidden in a hollow half a mile away to the west. Only rarely did Henry go to the northeast part of the pond—so rarely, in fact, that he visited a neighbor who lived there only once in seven months. When Thoreau did come to this northeast sector, he usually walked on the ice or rowed in his boat because there was no easy trail below the steep ridge.

After four stops in the northeast sector, we'll head west along the Pond Path to the northwest sector. There the theme is "Thoreau's World" of history. We'll find the authentic nineteenth-century land-scape where he slept, wrote his manuscripts, entertained visitors, hoed beans, chopped wood, docked his boat, bathed, swam, studied plants, climbed local hilltops, and meditated on nature. Aside from the well-trodden trails, this northwest sector is densely reforested woodland. The vast majority of Thoreau's observations in *Walden* came from this small corner of Walden.

The epicenter of Thoreau's historic landscape was his famous one-room house in the woods. That's where he slept at night and wrote every morning in solitude. During afternoons and evenings, he usually walked down the railroad tracks to town.

> Every day or two, I strolled to the village to hear some of the gossip which is incessantly going on there, circulating either from mouth to mouth, or from newspaper to newspaper,

and which, taken in homoeopathic doses, was really as
refreshing in its way as the rustle of leaves and the peeping
of frogs.

"Thoreau's World" includes six stops, more than in any other
sector. In sequence, Bare Peak, his favorite overlook, fronts a tall,
steep slope. Thoreau's Cove will be our entrance to his intimate sur-
roundings. Ecologically rich Wyman Meadow toggles back and forth
between being a lush meadow and a shallow part of the lake. The
House Site is the most important stop on our tour, marked by the
architectural footprint of his house and a cairn of stones built in
his honor. The Bean Field is the site of Henry's personal agricultural
experiment, his "commune" of one. Our Waterfront is what he called
his "pond-side," the clean gravel shore where he accessed the lake.

"Thoreau's World" is where a twenty-seven-year-old man, young
enough to be daring but mature enough to be serious, "went into
the woods to live deliberately." He went to create a philosophy of life
through thinking, reading, writing, and living simply in the midst of
nature. Shortly after his thirtieth birthday, in 1847, he left Walden
Pond with a rough first draft of *Walden* in hand. At that stage, his
manuscript was mainly a critique of society. He worked on two more
drafts through early 1849 until commercial failure as a writer forced
him to put his *Walden* project aside.

Nearly three years later, in late 1851, Thoreau began returning
to the pond, not to live, but to explore his former home turf as a
skilled, self-taught naturalist. By then, his former house was gone
and its cellar hole was suitable only for archaeology. At this stage
of his intellectual life, Thoreau was casting off his old role model,
Ralph Waldo Emerson, and modeling himself after the young
Charles Darwin, who had published the *Voyage of the Beagle* at age
thirty. This quickly became Thoreau's favorite book in his favorite
genre of scientific travel writing. Applying his newfound knowledge

of botany, zoology, geology, hydrology, limnology, and meteorology to the pond, and hauling a rowboat back to aid his studies, Thoreau saw his environment with fresh eyes. He returned to his abandoned *Walden* manuscript with new vigor, adding most of its eventual second half. The fusion of his earlier treatise, "Man and Society," with his later work, "Man and Nature," created his masterpiece.

Thoreau's method is suggested by an anecdote that found its way into the "Pond in Winter" chapter of *Walden*. When lying in bed one winter night, he heard the pond cracking and moaning beneath a blanket of snow. The muffled noises reminded him of sounds of restless overnight guests being troubled with "flatulency and bad dreams." When writing this up, Thoreau translated the physical sounds of the ice into the human sounds of companionship. He performed the same transcendental trick again and again at the pond, linking the physical attributes of different places to the different philosophical goals he was pursuing. In the process, his sense of place and his sense of self merged. Poet Robert Frost put it this way: "Think of the success of a man's pulling himself together under one one-word title. Enviable!" The one-word title Frost is referring to, of course, is Walden for the pond and *Walden* for the book.

With "Thoreau's World" behind us, our tour moves on to the southwest sector, where the theme is "Walden's Star." This large western basin of the lake is somewhat shaped like a five-pointed star with one of its points submerged. This sector gives us a chance to look back on "Thoreau's World" as a single large entity rather than as a cluster of six smaller stops. It also gives us a chance to experience the holistic radial symmetry of the western basin: "Wherever I sat," Thoreau wrote, "there I might live, and the landscape radiated from me accordingly."

"Walden's Star" has four stops. The first three are the tips of coves. Ice Fort Cove was the site of industrial-scale ice extraction and the westernmost point of Thoreau's pond survey. Sandbank Cove was half destroyed by earthen debris dumped into its tip during railroad construction. Deep Cove is where we will find the most perfectly shaped star point and the former site of a shantytown for immigrant Irish workers. Note that two of my cove names (Sandbank and Deep) do not match those on the official park map. At the last stop in this sector, Observatory, we will look back across the lake to see Thoreau's "forever new and unprofaned, part of the universe," a place with his "own sun and moon and stars."

Our backward look to "Thoreau's World" gives us a chance to reflect on his success capturing Walden in *Walden*.

Both Walden and *Walden* exude independence. Kettle ponds like Walden are usually separate from one another by virtue of their origin as sinkholes. Yet they are related to one another by occurring in clusters—in Thoreau's case, a "lake district" dominated by a "chain of ponds." Likewise, Thoreau found a "little world all to myself" when hunkered down inside the zone of kettle collapse only a slight distance away from his human tribe.

Walden and *Walden* exude simplicity. The star-shaped symmetry of the lake's western basin (where Thoreau made virtually all of his observations) gives the landscape a simple geometric elegance. In his chapter "The Ponds," he compared its concentric rings to the human eye with its pupil, iris, orbit, lashes, and brows. *Walden*'s thesis of "Simplicity, simplicity, simplicity!" matches the radial symmetry of the lake fronting his house.

Walden and *Walden* exude purity. The pond's extraordinary depth makes it a "deep and green well," exposing groundwater filtered by what is effectively finely crushed granite. The pond's broad surface area captures rain and snow straight from the sky. No streams that might bring in sediment or pollution enter the pond. The purity of

Walden's water kept Thoreau on track during his search for moral and ethical purity featured in his chapter "Higher Laws."

Thoreau walked the railroad tracks so often he was mistaken for an employee. View looks north toward Concord Station.

Walden and *Walden* exude sensitivity. The liquid membrane of Walden's surface was always rippling, sparkling, trembling, and shimmering at the slightest touch of nature. Wavelets from the touch of a raindrop, the dimple of a skater insect, or the nibble of a perch moved outward in widening circles until the ripples covered the pond. Thoreau was especially surprised at the sensitivity of the pond in late winter, when the cold, thick, rigid slab of ice responded acoustically to the slightest changes in air pressure and temperature. Likewise, Thoreau was constantly reminding himself to be fully awake and aware of everything taking place around him. In his chapter "Economy," he writes: "In any weather, at any hour of the day or night, I . . . stand on the meeting of two eternities, the past and future, which is precisely the present moment."

Walden and *Walden* exude resilience. The pond has proven itself extremely durable at long time scales. Gullies have not formed, owing to the excellent drainage of surrounding gravel soils. The water budget has remained exceptionally stable. The lake never dried up, and fluctuations in its water level remained within a twelve-foot range. In Thoreau's chapter "The Ponds," he claimed that Walden had hardly changed at all during the twenty years he'd been observing it. In fact, twenty generations of woodcutting had not destroyed the clarity of the water with clay, silt, and algae. The stony shore had resisted erosion, and its coves remained unconverted to marsh. Sedimentary archives from Walden's deep muck prove that the system had remained largely unchanged during the ten millennia prior to European colonization. Likewise, Thoreau's stamina and capacity for getting by without creature comforts were legendary among his peers. In "Where I Lived and What I Lived For," he declared that he "wanted to live so sturdily and Spartan-like as to put to rout all that was not life." Thoreau's clothing was similarly resilient. He preferred tough, drab corduroy and strong leather boots.

Walden and *Walden* exude renewal. In the book, *morning* is arguably the most important word. Each dawn was a personal renewal for Thoreau, each twenty-four-hour cycle an "epitome of the year." In his chapter "Spring," Thoreau's response to the yearly release of his lake from the grip of winter ice bordered on ecstatic.

Walking away from "Walden's Star" will bring us into the southeast sector, our fourth and final one. During "Re-entry," the historic landscape will slowly fade behind us as our modern world returns. When we reach the crest of the curve of Walden's southern shore, we will have reached Panorama, our culminating stop. There we will find the best view of the whole lake. This setting is also the best place for then-and-now comparisons between Thoreau's nineteenth-century past and our twenty-first-century present.

"Re-entry" is as much a mental process as it is a physical return—a chance to sum up and reflect on what we've learned. So, instead of adding more stops, our plan is for a brief walking meditation on the way back. As we walk quietly, the Pond Path loops south around the boat launch before turning north and disappearing amidst the sand and stonework of the Eastern Shore. Eventually, we'll reach the paved path where—fourteen stops earlier—we descended from the Terrace Edge. Ascending that same path and crossing the street will return us to the wooden ramp leading up to the Visitor Center. There, we will part ways.

## People

Henry David Thoreau (1817–1862) will be our silent companion at every stop. Although he was the star of the Walden Pond story, many other people played important supporting roles. Above all was Ralph Waldo Emerson (1803–1882), who converted a corner of his large country home, "Bush," into a library, office, study, and salon that became the epicenter of America's short-lived, but culturally potent, transcendentalism movement from which *Walden* emerged. Emerson was Thoreau's landlord, librarian, mentor, editor, banker, employer, and lifelong friend. This "sage of Concord" owned the woodlot on which his protégé built his small house. Emerson had the intellectual capital needed to promote Thoreau's posthumous legacy. Emerson's children and grandchildren inherited his love of nature and conservation ethic, which helped lead to the preservation of Walden Pond as public land.

Many other characters were part of the script. In 1653 an anonymous Puritan settler quilled "Walden Pond" on an early colonial document. In 1845 Thoreau's nearest neighbor was an alcoholic gardener named Hugh Coyle, who dropped dead on the road that October. In 1847 Henry watched Boston businessman Frederic Tudor convert the west end of Walden Pond into an industrial-scale

During the 1940s, Thoreau pilgrims often wore suits and long dresses. (Courtesy of the Thoreau Society, The Thoreau Society Archives at the Walden Woods Project's Thoreau Institute Library)

ice quarry for mining frozen water. In 1866, four years after Thoreau's death, George Heywood built an amusement park and picnic ground on Walden's western shore that catered to urban, Victorian-era tourists. In 1872 Mrs. Mary Newbury Adams from Dubuque, Iowa, inaugurated Thoreau's memorial cairn by placing a cobble at his House Site. In 1922 three Concord families (Emerson, Forbes, and Heywood) generously donated land, nucleating Walden Pond State Reservation. In 1948 famed architect T. Mott Shaw desecrated Thoreau's House Site with cut posts of quarried stone, a material that Thoreau detested for use in public monuments.

During my lifetime, the historical focus at Walden Pond has been on conservation. In 1957 Thomas B. Brennan, chairman of the Middlesex County Commissioners, launched a campaign to convert the natural pond into a community "bathtub," using bulldozers, ready-mix concrete, and imported sand. Fighting back was Edwin Way Teale, then president of the Thoreau Society. During the 1970s, public access to the park was scaled back to a maximum of 1,000 people at any one time to keep it from being ruined from overuse. In the 1980s, dozens of Thoreau die-hards and preservationists (Bradley Dean, Ed Schofield, Mary Sherwood, Tom Blanding, Walter Brain) fought back against a suburban "exit-ramp" culture threatening the ecosystem known as Walden Woods. From their fight emerged the Thoreau Country Conservation Alliance, which was succeeded in the 1990s by the Walden Woods Project (Don Henley, Kathi Anderson, and others). This project now oversees Thoreau's legacy in collaboration with the Massachusetts State Department of Conservation and Recreation, the Thoreau Society, the Concord Museum, the Concord Free Public Library, the Thoreau Farm Trust, and other groups.

And now, we have joined the never-ending story of Walden Pond. A portion of royalties from this guide supports the Friends of Walden Pond, the official, community-focused, fundraising arm of the Walden Woods Project.

## Questions

Following the model set by the venerable United States Park Service, the professional staff of Walden Pond State Reservation is committed to helping visitors learn about this nationally significant place. Staff interpreters guide group tours, help with teacher workshops, answer questions, and collaborate with partner organizations. Their Comprehensive Interpretive Plan, which was developed after extensive public review prior to opening the Visitor Center, poses three basic questions:

- *What makes Walden Pond a special place?*
- *What are the main stories to tell?*
- *What are the essential visitor experiences?*

Following Thoreau's belief that all true experience is an individual experience, each person's answers to these questions about the Walden experience will be unique and equally valid. Anyone who has previously toured Walden has probably already worked out answers to these questions. Others who have yet to tour Walden may find hints about what awaits from my three short answers for each of the three interpretive questions.

### What makes Walden Pond a special place?

Walden Pond is, first and foremost, the site of Thoreau's famous experiment in deliberate living. The steep wooded banks, the clear water, and the pond's roughly circular shape draw a visitor's attention inward and downward to a single focus. The management of Walden Pond State Reservation illustrates a successful compromise between pleasure-seeking recreation and stewardship-oriented conservation.

### What are the main stories to tell?

The beauty of nature is timeless. Henry David Thoreau did not live alone in a cabin in the *wilderness,* but he shared the pond with others and lived in full view of a busy railroad. *Walden* the book emerged from its author's self-identification with Walden the pond.

### What are the essential visitor experiences?

One essential experience is to see how clear the water is, despite two centuries of heavy use by up to half a million visitors per year. Another is to walk the circle of the Pond Path from modernity to history and back to modernity. A third is to make the pilgrimage to Thoreau's House Site in order to imagine him sitting on his doorstep, watching the sun sparkle over the distant face of the water.

## Using This Guide

This final section of the preparation explains how the elements of this book combine to create a coherent guide with a flexible range of options for different readers.

Four maps are printed on the inside covers for easy reference. They show the shape of the shore, selected landforms, the themes of our counterclockwise narrative, fifteen stops plotted on the official trail map, and a high-resolution shaded-relief topographic image revealing the lay of the land.

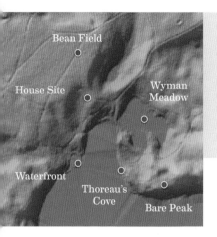

The six stops of "Thoreau's World" (northwest sector) are shown on a high-resolution topographic image created from LiDAR data. See maps for details. Thoreau's House Site overlooks a south-facing hollow. The actual Bean Field is farther east. Note rimmed hollow behind Waterfront. (Courtesy of the Massachusetts Office of Geographic Information)

Four timelines condense and simplify four histories. "Walden, the Author" is a partial biography of Thoreau's life, focused on his masterpiece. "*Walden,* the Book" is a timeline of publication and canonization. "Walden, the Place" is a chronology of human activity at the pond. "Walden, the Landform" is the geological narrative of the pond, including the powerful work of human beings.

The main part of this book is a counterclockwise tour around Walden Pond with fifteen stops. The Tour will pass through four geographic sectors, each with its own theme: "Our World" in the northeast, "Thoreau's World" in the northwest, "Walden's Star" in the southwest, and "Re-entry" in the southeast. Each of these sectors has its own short introduction.

The Tour follows the most efficient geographic sequence of stops. If efficiency were not a factor, however, we could visit the stops in a topical order. For example, a tour of Thoreau's biography would start at Terrace Edge, where the young boy David Henry (not yet Henry David) likely saw the pond for the first time. For literary history, the tour would start at Thoreau's Cove, where the transcendentalists of the 1830s ambled most often. For natural history, we would begin at the Boulder Wall, where Paleozoic rock is exposed. For poetry,

Smaller stones placed by visiting pilgrims on Thoreau's memorial cairn are being taken by visitors for souvenirs, leaving the larger ones behind. (See Stop 8, House Site.)

we would visit the center of the lake's largest basin, where Thoreau found a "lower heaven" unto itself, a veritable universe where the bottom was "pebbly with stars." Not having a boat, we will instead observe that center from the Observatory.

Each stop opens with a section called "At a Glance" that is brief enough to be read on site. As with a trail guide, this element helps the reader get located, oriented, and learn the main points. The longer text for each stop, "Sense of Place," opens with a summary, and then describes the stop in detail using a style modeled after travel literature. Some minor redundancy occurs between "At a Glance," the summaries, and the longer texts for "Sense of Place," so readers can opt to use any one of these elements and still get the main points.

Each of the longer texts zooms into two or more features. For example, Terrace Edge has a top and a bottom. Features zoom into details. For example, the memorial cairn (mound of stones) at Thoreau's House Site has an east and a west side. The eastern side is being eroded as tourists take away for souvenirs the pebbles and cobbles that international pilgrims have been bringing there for decades. The western side, however, is much more intact, being slightly less accessible. The difference between these two details (east vs. west) of one feature (cairn) at one stop (House Site) in one sector (northwest) illustrates the paradox of Walden Pond as a whole: the pond is simultaneously a place of historic conservation for the philosophical and a place of waterfront activities for the recreational. Balancing these bipolar goals is a never-ending management task for park officials and employees.

Each stop is also populated with the plants and animals Thoreau appreciated at that particular place. The ecosystem surrounding Walden Pond does not lend itself well to zooming in because it's broadly similar at all stops except one. The dry, acidic, fire-prone, infertile, and geologically young soils have repeatedly been cleared of their trees. This limits biodiversity. A more specific treatment of Walden's ecology is reserved for the stop Wyman Meadow, where the biodiversity is richest.

Illustrations are a mix of recent and historic photographs, as well as some artwork and a few drawings. Detailed captions ensure that each image can be understood on its own without reference to the text. This allows a reader to leaf through this book visually. All uncredited illustrations are my own.

Sidebars highlight information separate from the journey's narrative structure. There are seventy-five sidebars, five for each of fifteen chapters. The first four types of sidebars attach a relevant *Walden* quote to that stop. Place quotes (golden color) use Thoreau's words to describe the sight at the site. Animal quotes (burgundy) introduce the charismatic critters Thoreau encountered

Highbush blueberry (*Vaccinium corymbosum*). The picking of wild blueberries and huckleberries is an important literary theme in *Walden*. (See Stop 7, Wyman Meadow.) (© Ann Louise Hagevi/ Shutterstock)

at that stop, most of which remain in the park. Sound quotes (blue) describe something Henry heard at that stop. Plant quotes (brown) mention trees or shrubs that Thoreau linked to that stop. The final type of sidebar (gray) links a historic person to that particular stop. Each of these five types of sidebars is distinctly formatted, allowing the reader to cruise easily through the book based on their particular interests.

At the end of the tour, "Looking Back" takes advantage of our time together to reflect on Walden Pond in a new way. During our journey, we visited the stops in geographic order, learning whatever history and topics we could along the way. After visiting all the stops, we can revisit them in our minds in historical order, telling the story of the pond and its most famous resident.

# THE TOUR

Park Entrance

The sprawling headquarters of Walden Pond State Reservation are on a vast, flat terrace created by an ice-age river. The Visitor Center is located to the right. Stop 1, Simple House, is at the house replica. Stop 2, Terrace Edge, begins on the sidewalk to the left.

House Replica

# NORTHEAST: OUR WORLD

We've walked down the wooden ramp from the Visitor Center and are now heading toward our first stop on the stone dust path. Apart from the land itself, everything we see on the landscape—including the trees—has been either created or managed within the last century. In this sector, the theme is "Our World" of modernity.

Directly ahead—around either side of an island of trees—is our first stop.

## AT A GLANCE

**Object:** This small building is one of many twentieth-century replicas of Thoreau's original nineteenth-century dwelling. When being descriptive, he called it a house rather than a cabin, shack, hut, or shanty. Let's use the label he preferred.

**Location:** GPS coordinates 42° 26' 26.66" N, 71° 20' 05.52" W, 200 ft. The house is situated at the end of a stone dust trail about 100 yards north of the Visitor Center and about 20 yards east of State Highway 126 (Walden Street). The view is into the house, through the door or window.

**Moment:** In March 1845, construction of the original house began when Thoreau borrowed an axe, walked down the railroad tracks, and chopped down some vigorously growing white pines for the house's timber frame.

The replica (1985) of Thoreau's one-room house (1845) is located on the flat river terrace at park headquarters. Henry's original was in a hillside hollow to the west.

**Fun Fact:** Thoreau plastered his interior walls using fine, evenly textured white sand. The sand likely came from earthen debris dumped into the southwest corner of Walden Pond by immigrant Irish laborers building the Fitchburg Railroad.

**Nature:** Thoreau routinely fed the not-so-wild animals that lived with him in his house. He had a rabbit in the cellar, a jay under the eaves, and white-footed mice on his desk. In the fall, he let the wasps have their way.

# 1: SIMPLE HOUSE

## Sense of Place

*The faithful modern replica (1985) of Thoreau's original house (1845) was built on a flat wooded plain that was once the bed of a gravelly ice-age river flowing southwest. Thoreau's original was erected in a south-facing hollow with an open yard.*

The unusually cold and snowy winter of 1844–1845 was one of "discontent" for Henry David Thoreau. The twenty-seven-year-old bachelor was living with his parents, siblings, and boarders in a crowded house on Texas Street in Concord, Massachusetts. His transcendental friends were drifting apart. Their journal, *The Dial*, had recently gone out of print. He was still being publicly criticized for accidentally setting fire to about 300 acres of private woodland the previous spring.

So, on a cold blustery day in March, Henry borrowed an axe from his friend Bronson Alcott, walked

### Henry's house description

"I have thus a tight shingled and plastered house, ten feet wide by fifteen long, and eight-feet posts, with a garret and a closet, a large window on each side, two trap doors, one door at the end, and a brick fireplace opposite . . . I have also a small woodshed adjoining, made chiefly of the stuff which was left after building the house."

Architectural plans for this house replica were based largely on this description, supplemented by several other passages in *Walden*. The size of the house footprint was confirmed by the 1945 archaeological excavation by Roland Robbins.

## Woodland mice were Thoreau's frequent houseguests.

"The mice which haunted my house were not the common ones, which are said to have been introduced into the country, but a wild native kind not found in the village . . . When I was building, one of these had its nest underneath the house, and . . . would come out regularly at lunch time and pick up the crumbs at my feet. It probably had never seen a man before; and it soon became quite familiar, and it would run over my shoes and up my clothes . . . And when at last I held still a piece of cheese between my thumb and finger, it came and nibbled it, sitting in my hand, and afterward cleaned its face and paws, like a fly, and walked away."

Thoreau let the wild mice have free rein of his dwelling. They were intelligent, wild creatures rather than domesticated vermin. His species of mouse was probably the white-bellied or common deer mouse (*Peromyscus leucopus*), likely the most abundant wild animal in his woods. The sparse, dry ground cover and regular thick snowfalls created ideal habitat. The mice will eat almost anything, especially seeds, insects, fungi, and fruit, and normally keep out of sight by being nocturnal and living beneath the forest litter and snow. Their chief predators were other animals Thoreau enjoyed, including hawks, owls, minks, and foxes.

down the railroad tracks from his family home, trod through the woods to Emerson's woodlot, and began felling some "arrowy" white pines for timber. Though he had Emerson's permission to build, he claimed these saplings by "squatter's right," along with the shoreline stones and sand he would later dig up to use for his mortared foundation.

His young trees were about his age, having regrown like weeds from the slash of a previous clear-cut. They were just the right size for the six-inch-square timber posts and beams he would need for his house. Working amidst snow flurries, he sliced off the branches and hewed the thin logs into shape, leaving the bark on when he could. Like Thoreau, the young trees were oozing with the rising sap of spring following the torpid dormancy of winter. His hands became so sticky with resin that his lunch tasted of pine.

Replicas of his bark-covered timbers can be seen by looking up to the ceiling of this replica of the one-room, timber-framed house that Henry built elsewhere at Walden Pond and lived in between July 4, 1845, and September 6, 1847. By Thoreau's calculation, the interval was "two years, two months, and two days."

This small building—measuring fifteen feet long by ten feet wide by eight feet high at the ceiling—is by far the single most visited Thoreau-related stop at Walden Pond, undoubtedly because it's closest to the parking lots. Importantly, this house is not a copy of the one that Henry built because the exact details of the original are unknown. Instead, it's a reconstruction built by Roland Robbins in 1985 based on several independent lines of evidence.

First, it conforms to Thoreau's explicit and detailed description in the "Economy" chapter of *Walden*. With exactitude, he listed and accounted for every board and nail, most of which he bought secondhand. Next, we have his sister Sophia's sketch of the house's exterior, a likeness that was stylized and corrupted by the engraver before being reproduced for the frontispiece of *Walden*. We also have the "ground truth" measurements of Robbins, who confirmed the size and exact location of the house footprint, based on his excavation of its foundation in 1945. Finally, we have fragments of the original house now scattered in museum and private collections. Based on these four sources of information, Robbins drew up the plans for the building we're looking at and supervised its construction for the Thoreau Society. His architectural plans are available for purchase, making it possible for those inspired by Henry's example to build a replica of their own.

Simple House is to the original house as historic fiction is to history, or as biography is to an actual life. Things are missing. For example, Thoreau's original house, built only two years before he moved away, would have still emanated the smell of fresh-cut pine. In contrast, this decades-old replica has lost its distinctive "new" scent, and is so weather-beaten and tourist-worn that it feels like an old home, albeit a small one. Many details of the original remain unknown. Did it have kingposts? Was the front door off-center? Was the chimney inside or outside?

Most of the people visiting Simple House don't feel the least bit confined when they step inside.

> My dwelling was small, and I could hardly entertain an echo in it; but it seemed larger for being a single apartment and remote from neighbors. All the attractions of a house were concentrated in one room; it was kitchen, chamber, parlor, and keeping-room; and whatever satisfaction parent or child, master or servant, derive from living in a house, I enjoyed it all.

The interior is clean and neat, and surprisingly roomy, despite having a floor plan of only 150 square feet. The large glass windows and the open door offer a feeling of spaciousness enhanced by the dearth of furniture. Absent are window dressings, wall hangings, and dust collectors. Clutter is nonexistent. The impression is one of simplicity. This was not the case when Thoreau was working full throttle on his manuscripts. One wandering visitor found so many books and papers strewn about that he mistook it for a lawyer's office. Indeed, the house was more a writing retreat than anything else. Thoreau's most frequent visitor, William Ellery Channing, dubbed it a "wooden inkstand."

If we could have touched his interior walls, we could have felt how smooth the plaster was. That smoothness came from the fine texture of the sand mixed with the lime to make the plaster. Thoreau probably got his plaster sand from his "railroad sandbank" on Walden's southwestern shore, based on his description in *Walden:* "I brought over some whiter and cleaner sand for this purpose from the opposite shore of the pond in a boat, a sort of conveyance which would have tempted me to go much farther if necessary." Thoreau bypassed the natural shoreline sand he had used for his foundation mortar, which is almost always gritty and stained yellow with rust. Instead, for plaster, he wanted the pure, clean, white, well-sorted, evenly textured, and inorganic fine sand that is restricted to excavations cut deeply into the glacial lake sediments of the surrounding hills. In this case, Irish laborers working for the railroad had dug such sand from deep cuts into the nearby hills and then dumped it into Walden Pond to partially fill one of its coves. This means that the plaster Henry stared at while falling asleep came from the residues of industrial progress.

## The pattering of gentle rain on the roof

"The gentle rain which waters my beans and keeps me in the house today is not drear and melancholy, but good for me too . . . In the midst of a gentle rain while these thoughts prevailed, I was suddenly sensible of such sweet and beneficent society in Nature, in the very pattering of the drops, and in every sound and sight around my house, an infinite and unaccountable friendliness all at once like an atmosphere sustaining me . . ."

Inside Thoreau's house, under a wood-shingled roof and empty attic, the sounds of a summer rain would have been greatly amplified. One day the gentle sounds of a pattering rain moved Thoreau to see the natural world as a friendly, benevolent, and sustaining presence.

Thoreau purchased everything that went into his house, except for locally sourced materials such as wood, stone, and sand. In decreasing order of cost, he bought secondhand "sappy" boards used for exterior walls, one thousand used bricks for a chimney, a keg of nails, two secondhand windows complete with glass, two casks of manufactured lime, and miscellaneous other materials. Before winter, he had shingled his house "on the exterior down to the ground on every side." On the interior, he nailed lath boards between axehewn studs in order to plaster his walls with a fine white finish.

He furnished his house sparsely.

## Gray birch
### (*Betula populifolia*)

"Now only a dent in the earth marks the site of these dwellings, with buried cellar stones, and strawberries, raspberries, thimble-berries, hazel-bushes, and sumachs growing in the sunny sward there; some pitch pine or gnarled oak occupies what was the chimney nook, and a sweet-scented black birch, perhaps, waves where the door-stone was."

The removal of Thoreau's original house left a cellar hole "dent" in the woods. His dent and several others on Walden Street just north of the Simple House inspired him to chronicle the abandoned human community of Walden Woods. Birches readily sprout in the ruins of houses. His "black birch, perhaps" (not on the park inventory) was likely a gray birch, a locally documented, fast-growing weedy species that prefers coarse, dry upland soils with limited nutrients.

My furniture, part of which I made myself—and the rest cost me nothing of which I have not rendered an account—consisted of a bed, a table, a desk, three chairs, a looking-glass three inches in diameter, a pair of tongs and andirons, a kettle, a skillet, and a frying-pan, a dipper, a wash-bowl, two knives and forks, three plates, one cup, one spoon, a jug for oil, a jug for molasses, and a japanned lamp.

(A japanned lamp is one finished with a glossy black exterior copied from the lacquer finishes then commonly used in Japan.)

For a while, Thoreau kept three pieces of limestone on his desk. He then "threw them out the window in disgust," ostensibly because he claimed he "was terrified to find that they required to be dusted daily." More likely, he was angry with himself for failing to burn his own lime for mortar and plaster, an oversight that forced him to buy factory lime at great cost, undermining his sense of self-reliance. Throwing out these reminders of his failure makes logical sense and helped simplify his life.

Henry spent "nothing for curtains, for I have no gazers to shut out but the sun and moon, and I am willing that they should look in." An

open-flame fireplace heated his house for the first year. For the second winter, Henry bought a woodstove to reduce fuel consumption but lamented the loss of companionship the open fire provided.

Gray birch (*Betula populifolia*). This weedy species thrives on sunny, disturbed ground such as near old cellar holes. (© Bruce Heinemann/Photodisc/Getty Images)

The next winter I used a small cooking-stove for economy, since I did not own the forest; but it did not keep fire so well as the open fireplace. Cooking was then, for the most part, no longer a poetic, but merely a chemic process.

Famously, Thoreau wrote: "I had three chairs in my house; one for solitude, two for friendship, three for society." When "visitors came in larger and unexpected numbers" to this one-room house,

> they generally economized the room by standing up. It is surprising how many great men and women a small house will contain. I have had twenty-five or thirty souls, with their bodies, at once under my roof, and yet we often parted without being aware that we had come very near to one another.

Though Thoreau owned the house, he didn't own the land. So when Henry left Walden Pond on September 6, 1847, the landowner, Emerson, was charitable enough to buy the structure from him. Emerson then leased the house to his Scottish gardener Hugh Whelan, who hauled it away the following January. Lucky for us, Thoreau saved his furniture, most of which eventually ended up in the Concord Museum, where it remains on permanent display. My favorite piece of furniture is the small green desk he bought used for about a dollar. A true copy of this moss-colored desk remains inside the replica house today.

Before going outside, let's take a final look at all six of the interior surfaces: ceiling, floor, and four walls. Moving outside, we'll find four exterior walls and two roof pitches, all uniformly shingled. Having seen all twelve surfaces, we're now in a good position to decide whether this is a house or not. Thoreau certainly thought so, using that noun almost exclusively in *Walden*. There's a chimney built of a thousand bricks, four plaster walls, a tight floor of well-planed boards, a cellar, attic, and closet, casement windows, and a post-and-beam frame strong enough to hold together while dragged across town.

And if we can agree to call Thoreau's dwelling a house, then what kind of a house is it? I prefer the adjective *simple* over others (toy, tiny, small, one-room) because it's as general as it is accurate, and because achieving simplicity was one of Thoreau's most important goals.

Now that we're outside, let's fix our eyes on the square outline where the house meets the soil. All four corners lie at exactly the same elevation. They're part of a flat, vast, horizontal land surface below park headquarters that extends outward in all directions and continues beneath all seven of the large parking lots. Looking northwest toward Concord, the asphalt pavement of the highway is flat for a good half-mile. Looking southwest on the Lincoln side of the parking lots, the highway is flat as well.

This modern delta plain of the Rendu Glacier (Alaska) resembles the ancient delta plain on which park headquarters is located. In both cases, water and sediment issuing from a subglacial tunnel created a braided river delta that built outward into standing water. (Bruce Molnia, courtesy of the U.S. Geological Survey)

**Roland Robbins built the replica in 1985.**

Roland Robbins, a resident of nearby Lincoln, Massachusetts, and longtime member of the Thoreau Society, supervised the building of the Simple House. His claim to fame was the 1945 excavation of the original house foundation to commemorate the centennial of its 1845 construction. Robbins's excavation is described in his book *Discovery at Walden*. His work helped found the subdiscipline of historic archaeology.

This vicinity has not been graded flat by heavy construction equipment. Instead the flat surface was created naturally about 16,000 years ago as the broad floodplain of a large glacial river. Today that ancient riverbed is a broad gravel terrace standing about sixty feet above the level of Walden Pond. Thoreau was right to call this terrace a "shrub oak plateau."

What did park headquarters look like when the land was being created? Let's start by stripping away the trees, buildings, and solar panels, and then the organic forest soil down to bare gravel. Now imagine that we're standing on a low, flat-topped gravel bar, one of dozens rising above a braided network of shallow meltwater channels flowing to the southwest. This gravel surface was the top of what geologist J. Walter Goldthwait called the "Walden Delta" in 1905. This ancient riverbed, hereafter called the "ancient delta plain," was one of many built into an ancient glacial lake that has long since disappeared. Glacial Lake Sudbury was a ribbon-shaped body of cold, turbid water dammed up by the ice sheet receding to the north. The deltas built into it resemble those forming today in places such as Iceland and Alaska, where sediment-charged rivers emerge from beneath the edge of large glaciers and empty into standing water.

Half a century before Goldthwait mapped this ancient delta plain, Henry Thoreau had seen and understood its origin. In *Walden* he mused: "It was not always dry land where we dwell. I see far inland the banks which the stream anciently washed, before science began to record its freshets." In his *Journal,* Thoreau word-mapped the ancient delta plain as a flat riverbed that flowed between a "wide indentation in the hills" and "stretched away to the prairies of the west." He understood that his "shrub oak plateau" was "the ghost of the ample stream that once flowed to the ocean between these now distant uplands in another geological period." His "distant uplands" and "primeval banks" were the hills of Emerson's Cliff and the ridge of Bare Peak, where we will be four stops from now.

The glacial riverbed that Thoreau and Goldthwait mapped was abandoned when the ice margin retreated northward. By then, the original bedrock valley beneath Walden Pond had been filled up with sand below the glacial lake water line, and capped by bare gravel above it. The gravel was quickly covered with a treeless expanse of hardy plants called *tundra.* In succeeding millennia, this plant community was replaced by windswept shrubs, spruce-pine forest, mixed oak-pine forest, and, finally, the modern Walden Woods.

After leaving the Simple House, we will walk back in the direction of the Visitor Center. The path will take us past a bronze statue of Thoreau, a few kiosks with signs, and some benches made of split logs. Within a minute, we'll reach the painted crosswalk at Walden Street, a busy state highway where commuters back up during peak traffic. At the traffic signal, we'll push the button, wait for traffic, and cross the street to reach the sidewalk on the other side.

Though our eyes will be drawn westward out over the lake, we will turn around and face back in the direction of park headquarters to imagine a scene two centuries earlier.

PROHIBITED

## AT A GLANCE

**Object:** Note the drop-off between the flat terrace on which the Visitor Center was built and the steep slope below. This slope is the wall of a glacial kettle (type of sinkhole) that formed thousands of years ago when the land sank downward.

**Location:** GPS coordinates 42º 26' 25.22" N, 71º 20' 04.93" W, 197 ft. The stop is on the western (pond) side of the painted crosswalk crossing Highway 126. The stop contrasts views away from and toward the pond.

**Moment:** In June 1957 a convoy of heavy machinery, including bulldozers, cut a zigzag road down to the pond that was never used. The site was later restored and replanted with trees.

This stairway down the steep slope between Stop 2, Terrace Edge, and the pond was the main access before a paved pathway (the E-Ramp) was cut across the slope in the mid-twentieth century.

**Fun Fact:** The now-dilapidated and abandoned stairway above the bathhouse shows the steepness of the original access to the pond before excavation of the roadway down the bank.

**Nature:** All of the trees in this vicinity postdate Thoreau's era. Their predecessors were cut for firewood and timber during the winter of 1851–1852.

# 2: TERRACE EDGE

## Sense of Place

*Thoreau's first view of Walden Pond was likely from a dusty carriage road overlooking the east end of the pond. Though he was only a few years old, the memory always stayed with him. The lake he saw was created by gradual melting of buried glacial ice.*

The year is 1822. We're looking back in the direction of the Visitor Center, imagining what it looked like nearly two centuries ago. All the buildings, curbs, and pavements are gone. The trees are larger and the forest darker. Near what is now a well-engineered state highway was then a dusty, rutted carriage road weaving between the trees. Thoreau recalled the scene from a childhood memory: "In some places, within my own remembrance, the pines would scrape both sides of a chaise at once." The forest was spooky: "Women and children who were compelled to go this way to Lincoln alone and on foot did it with fear, and often ran a good part of the distance."

Suddenly, we hear the clip-clop of hooves and the squeaking of a horse-drawn buggy riding by. Thoreau, as a very young boy, was "in a chaise with his grandmother," traveling "along the shore of Walden Pond" to or from Weston. This scene, described by Frank Sanborn, Thoreau's friend and nineteenth-century biographer, strongly suggests that young David Henry (later Henry David) caught his first glimpse of Walden Pond from the Terrace Edge. Alternatively, his first view was of Thoreau's Cove, when his parents rented a horse

The flat surface (right) appeared as an elevated terrace when the colossal sinkholes of Walden Pond (left) formed. This view is from the headland between Ice Fort and Sandbank Coves.

and buggy in Boston so they could visit their home village and drive out Walden Street toward the pond: "When I was four years old, as I well remember, I was brought from Boston to this my native town, through these very woods and this field, to the pond. It is one of the oldest scenes stamped on my memory."

In either case, Thoreau likely would have seen the house of John Wyman, the potter on Walden Street just above the pond near the present crosswalk. Wyman had squatted there in the decades bracketing the American Revolution, living in a house with a view overlooking Walden Pond. The broken ceramic fragments—plates, bowls, and earthenware vessels—of his workshop can still be found today in the soil near his cellar hole. There was also a path down to the pond to what was called his "cottage landing." John Wyman's younger relative Tommy lived in that same house a generation later, and also owned a wood-lot across the road and nearer to town. This "Wyman Lot," so called, was the land that Ralph Waldo Emerson had purchased at auction in 1844 and where he let Thoreau build a house the following year. Tommy's successor in the house on Walden Street was an immigrant Scotsman named Hugh Coyle, who lived there with his wife until October 1, 1845, when he dropped dead on the road to town.

In late March 1845, Thoreau went out to the Wyman Lot to

## Henry's ancient river

"I have said that Walden [is] . . . directly and manifestly [related] to Concord River, which is lower, by a similar chain of ponds through which in some other geological period it may have flowed . . ."

Though not one of *Walden*'s most literary passages, this quote reveals that Thoreau understood that the "shrub oak plateau" surrounding Walden Pond was formerly the bed of an ancient river flowing southwesterly toward the Concord River. He also knew that Walden had "sunk" below that gravel riverbed to create what today we call a kettle pond.

begin building his house by cutting pines and hewing timbers. By mid-May, the house frame had been raised. By early June, Henry was returning daily to tend his beans. On July 4, he moved into his breezy house that was "merely a defence against the rain." Thoreau was thus a neighbor to Hugh Coyle for the first seven months of his Walden sojourn. Had Hugh not died, Thoreau could not have written his famously exaggerated opening line of *Walden:* "When I wrote the following pages, or rather the bulk of them, I lived alone, in the woods, a mile from any neighbor."

Though the two men lived for about three months above the same small lake, they saw practically nothing of each other. Socially, they were worlds apart. Thoreau was a Harvard-trained intellectual and a teetotaler. Coyle was an uneducated laborer, a "ditcher," and a heavy drinker. Henry visited his neighbor's house on this northeast rim of the pond only twice: once before Hugh died, and once to prowl through the debris of the dead man's life. The latter visit

## Chain pickerel were beautiful ambush predators.

"Ah, the pickerel of Walden! . . . I am always surprised by their rare beauty, as if they were fabulous fishes . . . They possess a quite dazzling and transcendent beauty which separates them by a wide interval from the cadaverous cod and haddock whose fame is trumpeted in our streets. They are not green like the pines, nor gray like the stones, nor blue like the sky; but they have, to my eyes, if possible, yet rarer colors, like flowers and precious stones, as if they were the pearls, the animalized nuclei or crystals of the Walden water."

The chain pickerel (*Esox reticulatus*) were the most revered fish of Walden. Fishing them for food took place mainly in winter. Men and boys came out from Lincoln and Concord via Walden Street, walked down the steep slope of the Terrace Edge, chopped holes through the ice, and dropped their lines. When Henry visited the fishermen, he found their catches of pickerel unusually beautiful. He noticed three varieties, perhaps because this species regularly hybridizes with others, such as the redfin pickerel (*E. americanus*) and the northern pike (*E. lucius*). Pickerel are ambush predators that lie in wait, striking quickly and powerfully with an open jaw equipped with backward-pointing, needle-sharp teeth. They are strongly cannibalistic when food is in short supply.

helped precipitate the *Walden* chapter "Former Inhabitants; and Winter Visitors," in which Thoreau identifies himself as part of a community living on the margin of Concord society.

The woods of the Terrace Edge were cut for firewood by landowner George Heywood in 1851–1852. What Thoreau described as a "sylvan amphitheater" got a lumberman's haircut. Heywood "hired workmen in an arrangement similar to one Thoreau describes" in *Walden,* writes historian Barksdale Maynard. "A woodcutter and assistant (paid a dollar daily) felled trees all winter at ten cents each, thirty or forty trees a day." The tools they used were a cross-cut saw, an axe, a beetle, and wedges. Their haul road to market was the primitive woods road between Lincoln and Concord, one that a thirty-four-year-old Thoreau called a "humble route . . . for the woodsman's team."

By 1879, however, this woods road was widened to

Chain pickerel (*Esox reticulatus*). This ambush predator is featured throughout *Walden*. (Duane Raver, courtesy of the U.S. Fish & Wildlife Service)

the Lincoln town line. One Concord summer visitor, Kate Tryon, called what is now Walden Street a "highway." By 1902, Mr. Warren of Lincoln was rumbling and bumping along what is now Route 126 in a horseless carriage, the first of many automobiles to come.

Now let's turn 180 degrees to look west out over the pond. Below us is a steep drop-off extending down the slope, into the water, and down to the bottom of the lake. Our Terrace Edge is the brink of a colossal sinkhole that opened up from below, punching a hole in what had been the flat ancient delta plain. Walden Pond was born when that slowly growing sinkhole widened and deepened to the point where it had sunk below the local groundwater table and began filling with seepage water.

This creation story highlights a popular misconception. Walden Pond doesn't *hold* surface water. Rather it *exposes* the groundwater of the surrounding sandy aquifer. Think of the basin of Walden Pond as a single, enormous, water-filled pore connected to billions of smaller pores between adjacent particles of sand. Thoreau was right to call Walden a "clear and deep green well" because that's exactly what it is: an oversized natural well.

The slope below Stop 2, Terrace Edge, was heavily eroded by swimmers during the 1920s prior to restoration. (Herbert W. Gleason, "Overlooking swimming beach at Walden Pond," August 24, 1924; courtesy of the Concord Free Public Library)

The fact that Walden Pond *exposes* groundwater explains why the lake can exist without inlet and outlet streams. Additionally, the surrounding sand and gravel is simply too permeable for significant surface runoff, even during the heaviest storms. This absence of runoff prevents the formation of surface rills, gullies, and streams. Instead of flowing sideways over the land, water soaks into the soil and trickles straight down through open pores. Eventually that infiltrated water reaches the zone of saturation at the water table. This addition of water from above raises the water table, which increases the water pressure within the aquifer, thereby forcing its water to flow sideways toward the pond through billions of pores. Walden Pond is so leaky it can't even hold the precipitation that falls on the lake. That increment quickly seeps sideways to the west or evaporates back to the sky from whence it came.

Thoreau understood these processes when composing *Walden*. "One value even of the smallest well is, that when you look into it you see that earth is not continent but insular. This is as important as that it keeps butter cool." This was his way of saying that, at depth within the Earth, there is "water, water, everywhere."

## The growling echoes produced by steep banks

"When, as was commonly the case, I had none to commune with, I used to raise the echoes by striking with a paddle on the side of my boat, filling the surrounding woods with circling and dilating sound, stirring them up as the keeper of a menagerie of his wild beasts, until I elicited a growl from every wooded vale and hillside."

Steep banks like that of the Terrace Edge return unusually strong echoes, especially when the leaves are off the trees. The three-basin shape of Walden crudely resembles the body of a guitar or violin.

The sinkhole origin of Walden Pond is broadly similar to that of sinkholes everywhere. Most simply, void space is created underground and the land surface descends into that void. At Walden Pond, the void space was created by the slow underground melting of masses of glacial ice that were left behind and buried by sediment.

But how did the stagnant ice get there? And why was it buried? Answering these questions requires turning the calendar back 25,000 years. Above Concord at the time was the Laurentide Ice Sheet, a dynamic solid mass several thousand feet thick that was creeping, sliding, and smearing its way toward its outermost edge at Martha's Vineyard. Then, about 22,000 years ago, the climate warmed. As the ice sheet thinned, its ragged, stagnant edge migrated northward, reaching the latitude of Concord about 16,000 years ago.

On upland hills, the stagnant ice melted straight down, leaving bare, stony soils. But in deeply shaded bedrock valleys like the one under Walden Pond, residual ice masses became isolated from one another and were quickly buried by sediment gushing out from the glacier edge. Burial by gravel saturated with icy water greatly delayed the rate of surface melting from solar heating. This gave the river time to bury the ice, and eventually to create a gravel plain.

### Shrub oak
#### (*Quercus ilicifolia*)

"The pitch pines and shrub oaks about my house, which had so long drooped, suddenly resumed their several characters, looked brighter, greener, and more erect and alive, as if effectually cleansed and restored by the rain."

Thoreau called the ancient river-bed above the Terrace Edge a "shrub oak plateau." He described his shrub oaks as "gnarled" oaks because the canopy is stunted and irregular, and the leaves are bristly like thorns. He considered the "shrub" oak and "bear" oak to be the same species. It prefers warm, dry substrates with limited nutrients, which explains its dominance on the dry gravel of the ancient delta plain above the lake.

One year, a shallow sag appeared on the surface. As the sag deepened, surface ruptures became visible. They linked up to form a shallow crater. Over centuries, that crater enlarged to become a growing sinkhole into which stones tumbled, gravel clattered, and mud flowed. When the sinkhole reached the water table, a shallow muddy pond was created. When it deepened further, a lake was born.

Thoreau knew this sinkhole story, writing: "Walden and other smaller ponds, and perhaps Fairhaven, had anciently sunk down" below the ancient delta plain because the "level" of the "shrub oak plain is continued in many cases even over extensive hollows." He also knew that the sinkholes were likely glacial in origin: "It looks as if the snow and ice of the arctic world, travelling like a glacier, had crept down southward and overwhelmed and buried New England." But because the glacial theory was highly controversial in his day, Thoreau substituted a delightful allegory in place of geology:

... anciently the Indians were holding a pow-wow upon a hill here, which rose as high into the heavens as the pond now sinks deep into the earth, ... and while they were thus engaged the hill shook and suddenly sank ... It has been conjectured that when the hill shook, these stones rolled down its side and became the present shore.

These modern glacial kettles (Bering Glacier, Alaska) are still melting down. They resemble the kettles of Walden Pond during an early stage of creation. (Bruce Molnia, courtesy of the U.S. Geological Survey)

Thoreau finished his allegory with one of his famous puns about the origin of the name *Walden:* "I detect the paver. If the name was not derived from that of some English locality—Saffron Walden, for instance—one might suppose that it was called originally Walled-in Pond." In this case the pond was *walled in* by stony sinkhole slopes.

Walden Pond is a kettle lake, the world's most famous example of this type. The label *kettle* was introduced by American glacial geologists shortly after Thoreau's era to describe basins shaped like the namesake cooking vessel. Technically, kettles are depressions or hollows of the land surface, created when sediment deposited on or near stagnant ice collapses downward and inward to create a depression. This origin gives rise to isolated lakes that have steep banks, dry soils, filtered water, and crudely circular shapes, and that lack inlet and outlet streams. These general characteristics fit the particulars of Walden Pond perfectly.

Thoreau shares his observations in his chapter "The Ponds."

### Hugh Coyle was a neighbor in 1845.

Hugh was one of thousands of Irish immigrants in Greater Boston who worked as a laborer, in his case a "ditcher" who drained swamps and meadows. He was one of the poor town residents who was addicted to alcohol. The Wyman house, now a cellar hole, is located on the Terrace Edge near the park entrance. Coyle—Thoreau spelled his name Quoil—was living in that house when Thoreau began building his own above Thoreau's Cove. The two men were distant neighbors at the pond for seven months until Coyle collapsed on the road and died.

This pond is so remarkable for its depth and purity as to merit a particular description. It is a clear and deep green well, half a mile long and a mile and three quarters in circumference, and contains about sixty-one and a half acres; a perennial spring in the midst of pine and oak woods, without any visible inlet or outlet except by the clouds and evaporation.

At Walden, the result of kettle formation was a landform resembling an oversized sports stadium sunk below many surrounding acres of gravel parking lots and half-filled with water. As with every stadium, the view slopes inward and downward onto a playing field.

> A field of water betrays the spirit that is in the air. It is continually receiving new life and motion from above. It is intermediate in its nature between land and sky . . . It is remarkable that we can look down on its surface. We shall, perhaps, look down thus on the surface of air at length, and mark where a still subtler spirit sweeps over it.

*Kettle* is a general term geologists use for any meltdown basin, whether large or small, whether dry or wet. *Kettle hole* is reserved for a small kettle that's dry for much or all of the year. *Kettle pond* and *kettle lake* refer to a kettle of any size that has perennial standing water. These last two terms are synonyms, with *pond* being the New England vernacular, and *lake* being preferred out West.

Walden Pond was named by the English Puritans of the mid-seventeenth century. Their word *Walden* likely derived from the *Weald*, a wooded region of southeast England. In their lexicon, the word *pond* was reserved for small to mid-sized bodies of water rimmed by vegetation. The word *lake* was reserved for the rockier, rougher, and more elongated bodies of water, like the lochs (lakes) of Scotland or those of the highland English Lake District.

In late-nineteenth-century Concord, railroad entrepreneurs and many local residents rechristened the Puritan name "Walden Pond" into the American name "Lake Walden" to more effectively market this body of water as a recreational resource. In the twentieth-century United States, environmental regulators independently adopted the word *lake* for any permanent body of fresh water ten acres or larger, regardless of its appearance. At 62 acres, Walden Pond is thus a lake six times over.

Thoreau skillfully wove the distinction between pond and lake into *Walden*. His remove from society was to a geographic place, a pond. His experience of that place was with a large body of clean water, a lake. Thoreau generally used *pond* when referring to place, and *lake* when describing the attributes of that place. When writing "This is my lake country," he was emulating the Lake Poets of the English Romantic tradition. When declaring Walden Pond and White Pond to be twin "Lakes of Light," he was referring to their common attributes, and not to geographic places.

Thus, Walden Pond is a lake, one that expanded over four distinct kettles, hereafter called *basins*. The eastern, central, and western basins refer both to the shape of the bottom and to the lake surface above those deep depressions. Walden's fourth basin, named after Wyman the potter, joins and leaves the other three basins depending on the height of the groundwater table, which rises and falls.

The Terrace Edge we're standing on is the broadly curved margin of the kettle that formed the eastern basin. The steep slope here was originally nearly straight from the brink to the bottom of the lake. Today it's a curved profile, its upper half covered by forest soil and a stand of trees, its lower half covered by water. Prior to the middle of the twentieth century, swimmers walked down this steep bank on either eroded trails or concrete stairs to a shoreline with a narrow beach fronting a steep drop-off.

Today, the overwhelming majority of visitors to Walden Pond take the concrete pavement pathway known as the "E-Ramp" (short for emergency ramp) that cuts obliquely across the face of the slope. Walking down this path, we'll quickly lose sight of the highway above us because our line of sight to the east will be blocked by the wall of the kettle. Instead we will see, exposed between the tree roots, rust-stained pebbles and cobbles of river gravel.

At this point, it's informative to walk a few steps back up the paved path to bring the flat terrace back into view, and then walk a few steps back down inside the kettle to make it disappear again.

What we're doing is bobbing up and down from the ancient delta plain to the more secluded hollow. Thoreau experienced this same transition whenever he came and went from his house in the woods. This is a critical insight that most visitors miss. The vast majority of Henry's *Walden* experiences took place when he was hunkered down inside a deep and colossal kettle, looking farther down to the lake surface.

It's time to walk the E-Ramp all the way down to the bottom of the slope. There we'll find ourselves on an extensive patio of quarried flagstone and cement. After walking on it for a hundred feet or so, turn right to take one of several low stairways down to the beach. Our next stop is at the water's edge.

## AT A GLANCE

**Object:** The vast waterfront of stone and sand was engineered nearly from scratch during the twentieth century. As late as 1903, the beach was a short, narrow strip of pebbly sand.

**Location:** GPS coordinates 42° 26' 21.98" N, 71° 20' 05.14" W, 154 ft. The engineered beach parallels the entire east end of Walden Pond below park headquarters, making it impossible to miss.

**Moment:** On the hot day of July 14, 1935, pond historian W. Barksdale Maynard reported that the Walden crowd reached 35,000. This number staggers belief.

Walden's entire Eastern Shore is an engineered beach backed up by an architectural hardscape that includes a shingled concrete bathhouse.

**Fun Fact:** Visitation for waterfront recreation spiked first when personal automobiles were invented in the early twentieth century and second when the Highway 2 bypass opened in the early 1930s.

**Nature:** Nowhere else on Walden Pond has the battle between landscape preservation and recreational development been more pitched. Thoreau's battle of the ants provides an interesting allegory for this continuing conflict.

# 3: EASTERN SHORE

## Sense of Place

*The wide beach, bathhouse, stone patio, stairways, and stone walls that line the Eastern Shore of Walden Pond were designed and built during the twentieth century. When Thoreau lived at the pond, the shore was a short, narrow beach.*

We're standing at water's edge, looking west. In January 1846, Thoreau stood in nearly the same spot looking out over snow-covered ice thick enough to support a team of horses. After mounting his brass surveying compass on a wooden-legged tripod, he sighted down the full length of the lake to the tip of Ice Fort Cove. We'll be there eight stops from now, looking back in this direction.

Henry's anonymous assistant was out on the ice, following hand signals and moving away to trace out a straight line on the snow. Following that line, Thoreau later used an archaic type of surveying chain (Gunter) to precisely measure the length of the lake. Stretching his chain taut over each segment, he summed up the length of Walden Pond to be 173.5 rods, each 16.5 feet long. This translates to a length of 2,863 feet, or 0.54 miles. Using a different technique called *triangulation,* he mapped the pond perimeter and measured it to be 1.7 miles.

At specified distances, Thoreau chopped holes in the ice to fathom the depth of the water and the firmness of the bottom. This he accomplished by dropping a fist-sized stone tied to the end of

Walden Pond (center) is part of a "chain of ponds." All formed as glacial kettles below a sediment-filled ancient valley (dashed white lines). Sandy Pond (the largest lake in the photo) is not a kettle. The Sudbury River (left) and Concord Center (top) are also shown. (GoogleEarth)

a fishing line. The depth at each hole was the distance it took for the line to go slack. The firmness of the bottom was determined by how quickly the line went slack: abruptly for firm sand and more slowly for gelatinous muck.

From these measurements and observations, Thoreau determined that the bottom of Walden Pond consisted of three separate sinkholes, or kettles, or basins that were rimmed by sand and centered by muck. In *Walden* he illustrated all three basins on his east–west survey profile. If the present groundwater table were to drop sixty feet, the large lake of today would shrink down into three separate ponds crudely aligned with Henry's larger "chain of ponds." This larger chain of ponds follows the buried bedrock valley that was filled to overflowing by glacial sediments before the kettle ponds formed.

When Thoreau stood at the Eastern Shore more than a century ago, his view was radically different from what we can see today. Thick slabs of ice were being thrust above one another on a steep, narrow shore. Trees were being rubbed raw by jostling floes. The beach was short and narrow, even in summer. Today, the winter ice is rarely thick enough to thrust, the trees and the former hillside have been excavated away, a wide engineered beach runs the full length of the Eastern Shore, and the sand is backed up by an unbroken hardscape of cement and stone. Specific architectural features include a boat launch, a two-story concrete bathhouse, a continuous rim of stone walls, and several sets of rickety stairs, one of which is now chained off for safety's sake.

In his chapter "The Ponds," Thoreau gives a good general description of the entire mid-nineteenth-century lake perimeter: "The shore is composed of a belt of smooth rounded white stones like paving-stones, excepting one or two short sand beaches, and is so steep that in many places a single leap will carry you into water over your head." The trivial amount of sand beach he noted makes perfect sense to natural scientists because the lake surface lies deeply sheltered below the regional wind, and because the pond's steep banks create wave conditions favorable for dragging beach sand into deeper water. The stone-paved shore also makes sense, given the dearth of sand and the weight of thick ice shearing back and forth over the nearshore zone.

One of Thoreau's two short beaches was a "smooth sandy beach" at the "sandy eastern shore." Visitor Kate Tryon described this same beach in the 1890s as a narrow "pebbly beach." Photographer H. W.

## The audible cracking of lake ice

"The pond began to boom about an hour after sunrise, when it felt the influence of the sun's rays slanted upon it from over the hills; it stretched itself and yawned like a waking man with a gradually increasing tumult, which was kept up three or four hours. It took a short siesta at noon, and boomed once more toward night, as the sun was withdrawing his influence."

The thick ice of late winter was a rigid solid that expanded and contracted as the temperature changed. The inevitable ruptures made a variety of sounds, which were loudest where the length of the ice was the greatest. The Eastern Shore faces the longest extent of ice.

In 1903, Walden's Eastern Shore had a short, narrow, pebbly beach. Swimmers are standing on a raft to the right.
(Herbert W. Gleason, "Swimming beach at Walden, Concord, Mass.," May 30, 1903; courtesy of the Concord Free Public Library)

Gleason described this same beach in 1903 as "the thinnest strip of sand." Today, it's a vast stretch of imported glacial sand that widens every year.

The popularity of this beach as a "swimming place" at the eastern end of Walden Pond began in 1899 when a raft equipped with diving boards—a "float and spring board"—was installed at what the locals called "Sandy Beach." Some entrepreneur published an advertisement to bring swimmers here, with the idea that construction costs could be recouped with an entrance fee. The owner of this land, George Heywood, didn't seem to care. His interest lay with the dollar value of cordwood timber on its slopes.

During the first decade of the twentieth century, the rapid proliferation of the personal automobile rendered Walden's small swimming beach accessible via Walden Street. By 1913 the town of Concord was conducting swimming lessons at the eastern end of what was then a de facto public swimming beach. By 1917 they had added bathhouses with dressing rooms and toilets, and a policeman was hired to keep the peace.

The year 1922 was the second most critical year of pond history, following 1845, the year that Thoreau built his house. Noticing that townspeople were enjoying wholesome outdoor activities, the Emerson, Forbes, and Heywood families donated much of the lake perimeter to the state. What had been private woodlots and family picnic places became a public park called Walden Pond State Reservation. Because the state had no agency to administer the land, jurisdiction dropped down to the county level. The

## Henry's tiny beach at what is now the Eastern Shore

"The shore is composed of a belt of smooth rounded white stones like paving-stones, excepting one or two short sand beaches, and is so steep that in many places a single leap will carry you into water over your head."

The present wide beach, extensive shallow zone, and architectural hardscape runs continuously along the entire Eastern Shore of Walden Pond. None of this was there when Thoreau described the scene in the 1840s and 1850s, or when it was photographed by H. W. Gleason in 1903.

Middlesex County Commissioners were put in charge. Their management style prioritized recreational beach access and gave little thought to conserving the cultural landscape. Under their charge, which spanned the decades prior to widespread air conditioning, Walden Pond became a hyper-popular summer swimming facility.

In 1924, H. W. Gleason photographed the Eastern Shore from the Terrace Edge. His photo (see page 52) shows heavily eroded slopes, blowing litter, and a large crowd. In response to these problems, the commissioners covered the slopes with extensive lawns and built several broad walkways. They also lengthened the broadened beach to 450 feet and built a massive raft 80 feet long and 40 feet wide with a diving board on each side.

The rerouting of U.S. Route 2 in 1931 brought Walden Pond's swimming facility within 750 feet of a major highway. The yearly total was estimated to be 483,000 swimmers. During the 1930s, a

## Speckled alder

*(Alnus incana* ssp. *rugosa)*

"These alders loomed through the mist at regular intervals as you walked half way round the pond."

The speckled alder almost certainly grew out over the narrow nineteenth-century sand-pebble beach before it was hacked away during the twentieth century to make room for the Eastern Shore. Alder is a fast-growing shrublike tree that requires lots of sun. Its shallow root system makes it common on lakeshores, riverbanks, and wetlands where the water rises and falls. Thoreau mentions it frequently in *Walden*.

hardscape became necessary to handle the foot traffic of an estimated 10,000 to 20,000 people per summer weekend. Our walking trail, the Pond Path was cut around the lake to deconcentrate heavy use of the Eastern Shore. During the 1940s, the county commissioners decided to lengthen the beach to cover the entire Eastern Shore and to truck in tons of concrete. The two-story concrete bathhouse was built in 1947. It's still there today, though beautified by a façade of wooden shingles. Visitation remained high into the 1950s, with up to 35,000 swimmers per hot weekend in 1952.

The third most important year in pond history was 1957. Pushed by relentless demand, and with approval and funding from the state legislature, the Middlesex commissioners decided to upgrade once again. Chainsaws buzzed on every bank. Hundreds of trees were cut down. Bulldozers rumbled in shallow water. A zigzag road was cut down to the pond. The banks were cut away to make room for "blacktop parking" adjacent to the water. Continued importation of sand widened the main beach drastically. Another new beach, Red Cross Beach, was created from scratch by excavating the sunny northeastern bank, a shore Thoreau called his "fireside." His fireside was completely erased. The icing on the commissioner's recreational cake was a concrete pier extending more than a hundred feet out into the water. This aggressive makeover of the pond in 1957 was consistent with the mood of Concord residents at the time. The following year

they voted 603 to 38 to create a vast garbage dump less than a thousand feet north of the lake shoreline. Luckily, its toxic leachate drains the other way, though this was not known when the dump was sited.

This 1957 photograph shows the creation of Red Cross Beach from what had been a steep, wooded hillside that Thoreau called his "fireside." (Keith Martin, "Destruction of shore at Walden," showing sand piles and trucks; courtesy of the Concord Free Public Library)

The 1957 Annual Gathering of the Thoreau Society started just a few days after the commissioners began their assault on the pond. The Thoreauvians were so shocked and appalled that they immediately created a "Save Walden Committee" and filed an injunction to stop the destruction. After three years of continuous litigation and conflict, the Massachusetts State Supreme Judicial Court finally ruled in 1960 that the Middlesex County Commissioners had indeed violated the terms of the deed creating the reservation,

Ants (no species assigned). Thoreau's battle of the ants in his chapter "Brute Neighbors" is an allegory for the war between recreationists and conservationists. (© Niroot Sampan/IStockphoto.com)

which required preserving the "Walden of Thoreau and Emerson." Concrete piers and lakeside parking lots, the court decided, were inconsistent with the deed restrictions.

After that turning point, the Middlesex County Commissioners began to prioritize conservation along with recreation. This policy shift was aided by the 1962 designation of Walden Pond as a National Historic Landmark, a prelude to passage of the Wilderness Act by the U.S. Congress in 1964. The political appeal of wilderness preservation followed Thoreau's axiom: "In Wildness is the preservation of the world."

During the 1970s, the responsibility for conserving Walden Pond was transferred from Middlesex County to the newly created Massachusetts Department of Natural Resources. A further tilt from conservation to preservation took place during the 1980s when Walden was tucked into an even newer agency, the Department of Environmental Management. They removed much of the intrusive infrastructure, including the concrete pier and two older bathhouses, which were gone before my initial visit in 1985. They also upgraded the landscaping by improving the stone patio and shingling the concrete bathhouse.

After six decades of limited maintenance, the Pond Path had become a disaster of erosion, collapse, and public safety hazards. So, during the 1990s, the entire trail was bordered by heavy-gauge wire fence and stabilized with a

## Red and black ants at war

"One day when I went out to my woodpile, or rather my pile of stumps, I observed two large ants, the one red, the other much larger, nearly half an inch long, and black, fiercely contending with one another . . . Looking farther, I was surprised to find that the chips were covered with such combatants, that it was not a *duellum*, but a *bellum*, a war between two races of ants, the red always pitted against the black, and frequently two red ones to one black . . . On every side they were engaged in deadly combat, yet without any noise that I could hear, and human soldiers never fought so resolutely."

*Walden*'s battle of the ants is a widely studied literary allegory for human wars. At the Eastern Shore, Thoreau's ant war (1845–1847) is a stand-in for the land-use war (1957–1960) between recreational development (Middlesex County Commissioners) and historic conservation (Save Walden Committee). For three years, those fighting for enhanced recreational swimming facilities battled fiercely with those fighting to preserve the "Walden of Thoreau and Emerson." Ants are important ecosystem engineers of terrestrial ecosystems such as Walden Woods. Thoreau was fascinated by their social behaviors and earth-moving capabilities.

host of engineering solutions. At dozens of sites above the lakeshore, large blocks of rough-cut stone were hauled in to control erosion

**Kate Tryon described the beach in 1890.**

Miss Tryon was an artist and ornithologist who spent summers in Concord at the home and studio of noted sculptor Daniel Chester French on Sudbury Road and frequently tramped Walden Woods in search of the haunts of Henry Thoreau. In 1890, she described only a thin "pebbly beach" at the Eastern Shore. In 1895, she organized "An Evening with Thoreau" by decorating French's studio with Thoreau's favorite plants, exhibiting her watercolors, and speaking to a crowd of seventy-five people. Interest in Thoreau was clearly on the rise in Concord by the close of the nineteenth century.

and to convert steep, dangerous gullies into stairways, some of which have since collapsed. Retaining walls built from old railroad ties were installed to prevent bank erosion. Mary Sherwood, an ardent conservationist, led the effort to replant trees on the degraded banks, especially to the northeast where a road had previously been cut down to the pond.

Before leaving the Eastern Shore, we would benefit by reflecting on a recent and important phenomenon: the recognition that human beings have become geological agents on par with the ice sheet responsible for the previous landscape transformation. Effectively, we've launched a new geological epoch called the Anthropocene. The continuing makeover of the Eastern Shore is a perfect example. Every year, imported "sand is added to a created beach in the early spring." A large portion of that sand then washes into the pond during summer storms, shrinking the size of Walden Pond.

A 1999 water study by the U.S. Geological Survey highlights an even greater, though invisible, impact. Scientists found elevated levels of nitrate seeping into the lake near the center of the main swimming beach. This pollution was leaching from the septic drain field used by park headquarters and traveling under the highway as a plume within the groundwater. The scientists also learned that the number one source of phosphorous pollution during summer was human urine. Happily, the leachate problem has been fixed. Unhap-

pily, nobody has yet found a way to enforce a rule against peeing in the water.

The broad beach at Walden's Eastern Shore widens from runoff following heavy storms. This is a smaller-scale version of what the original ancient delta plain used to look like: flat and sandy with bars and braided channels. (Patrick Morgan)

Facing the lake, we now turn 90 degrees to the right and walk north, back toward the bottom of the paved pathway that we walked down from the Terrace Edge. There we will find stone walls built of local boulders and capped by cement. Our next stop can be located anywhere near the north end of that wall.

## AT A GLANCE

**Object:** Above the beach is a continuous wall built of stones, mortar, and concrete. The northern part of this wall is the best place on the tour to see the natural boulders and cobbles that are widely distributed throughout the nearby hills and that once lined the shore of Walden Pond.

**Location:** GPS coordinates 42° 26' 23.54" N, 71° 20' 04.96" W, 157 ft. The stop can be anywhere the rock of the boulders and cobbles is clearly exposed. These coordinates are for the place of the photograph above.

**Moment:** In March and April 1845, Henry Thoreau gathered several cartloads of stones similar to the ones we see in these walls and hauled them up to his House Site to build a foundation for his dwelling.

Three segments of stone walls were built to stabilize the excavated slope below the paved pathway leading down to Walden Pond from Stop 2, Terrace Edge. Stop 4, Boulder Wall, is to the lower right.

**Fun Fact:** On Thursday morning, July 25, 1878, twenty-seven large cobbles, like those in this stone wall, were carried up from Walden's shore, inscribed with pilgrims' names, and ceremoniously placed on a cairn of stone to mark Thoreau's House Site.

**Nature:** These dry, exposed boulders provide a habitat so limiting that typically only lichens and microbes grow on them. Thoreau loved lichens for their beauty, simplicity, and tenacity.

# 4: BOULDER WALL

## Sense of Place

*The line of stone walls between the beach and the wooded bank shows us the materials Thoreau used to build his house foundation. The stones also provide clues to New England's ancient landscapes of fire and ice.*

Perhaps there will be rain or fog when you visit. Wetness brings out the colors of stone and enhances the contrasts because the clinging film of water reduces the scattering of light from rough surfaces and refracts light into crevices. The result is a more vivid, almost magnified look.

Now let's feast our senses on the stones. There are colors: pinks, grays, black, greens, tans, and other earth tones. There are patterns: massive, blotchy, and layered. There are textures: rough, smooth, and polished. There are shapes: chunks, balls, disks, ovals, and slabs. And finally, there are details: lines and curves, sharp and round corners,

### Henry's bedrock reality

"Let us settle ourselves, and work and wedge our feet downward through the mud and slush of opinion, and prejudice, and tradition, and delusion, and appearance . . . till we come to a hard bottom and rocks in place, which we can call reality."

Thoreau used rock to symbolize fundamental truth. He also enjoyed thinking about how his world formed. He knew the names of the rock types exposed in the Boulder Wall, and he also figured out most of the local geology.

points and holes. These are the stones of New England. Let's rub them with our fingers. Some are as smooth as glass, while others are as rough as coarse sandpaper. Let's smell them. Let's enjoy their silicate chemistry before we perform the transcendental trick of turning stones into spiritual symbols.

But let's first clarify a significant point. Stones are not the same as rocks. Rock is a material. Stones are objects made from that material, the objects used to build this wall. Similarly, wood is a material. Timbers are objects made from that material, the objects Thoreau used to frame his wooden house.

To build his house foundation, Thoreau hauled stones and sand up from the shore, made mortar by mixing that sand with lime, stacked those stones above one another, and mortared everything together. The resulting stone foundation supported the timber sills and frame of his house, which supported the shell of boards, the sheath of shingles, and the plaster walls, all of which supported his life and his writings.

Rock is Earth's most fundamental material. This is why, during his search for what is real and what is phony, Thoreau settled on rock as the final arbiter of truth.

> Let us settle ourselves, and work and wedge our feet downward through the mud and slush of opinion, and prejudice, and tradition, and delusion, and appearance, that alluvion which covers the globe, through Paris and London, through New York and Boston and Concord, through Church and State, through poetry and philosophy and religion, till we come to a hard bottom and rocks in place, which we can call reality . . .

In fact, following his 1846 excursion to Maine's Mount Katahdin, Thoreau concluded that all of "our life in nature," boils down to rock:

"the solid earth! the actual world! the common sense!" Even his dreams, he realized, were grounded by rock and stone: "If you have built castles in the air, your work need not be lost; that is where they should be. Now put the foundations under them."

Indeed, everything in his world originally came from rock: the stones of his house foundation, the mineral soil that grew the timbers of his house, and the mineral water that grew the bones that hefted his axe. "There is nothing inorganic," Thoreau wrote in one of *Walden*'s most important lines. Indeed, the boundary between life and

These boulders were milled from jagged blocks of ancient rock into rounded shapes by moving glacial ice and meltwater streams. Modern weathering and human construction are also geological agents.

nonlife is fuzzier than generally assumed. Ours is a living earth experiencing continuous creation above its ultimate raw material, rock. Earth's crust is always in the process of being recycled from rock to stone to animated life to sediment, and then back to rock again. All of Earth's water, including Walden Pond, had been steamed out of our nascent rocky planet when it was being born.

Let's imagine the Boulder Wall we're seeing as a diorama in a natural history museum. For the careful observer, such an exhibit can

Great horned owl (*Bubo virginianus*). For Thoreau, the great horned owl signified ancient wisdom. (© Peter Burian/Corbis)

explain the entire history of Walden Pond, not merely the story of the last century or two. Quoting one of my earlier books:

> Stone walls hold time like a set of Russian dolls. The smallest doll, the one farthest inside, contains the oldest things in the universe, the elements. Outward dolls, in succession, are the minerals composed of the elements; the stones composed of the minerals; the wall composed of stones; and the modern, weathered surface, which is a blend of everything. All of this time is contained in every stone.

## The great horned owl symbolized pre-human consciousness.

"I was also serenaded by a hooting owl . . . Hoo hoo hoo, hoorer hoo . . . I rejoice that there are owls. Let them do the idiotic and maniacal hooting for men. It is a sound admirably suited to swamps and twilight woods which no day illustrates, suggesting a vast and undeveloped nature which men have not recognized. They represent the stark twilight and unsatisfied thoughts which all have."

Thoreau's "hooting owl," which he also called a "cat owl," was the great horned owl (*Bubo virginianus*). For Thoreau, the hoot owl represented the "vast and undeveloped nature" of the world before the dawn of human cognition, whose ancient story is told by the stones of the Boulder Wall. Great horned owls are the largest and most powerful of the common owls, with a wingspan up to five feet. As nocturnal ambush predators, they depend on exceptional powers of sight and hearing. They migrate seasonally.

The preceding quote identifies five critical stages in New England's landscape history. In *Walden,* Thoreau differentiated them all. His narrative begins with what he called the elemental "rain" of planetary particles, meaning the cosmic dust, asteroids, and comets that accreted together under the influence of gravity to create planet Earth. Next, he enjoyed thinking about Earth's internal geothermal "furnace," which he knew had created the rock from which his New England landscape had been carved. Next, he contemplated the shaping of the land during the glacial epoch, which he cryptically referred to as the "diluvial" period. Next came the Puritans who settled historic Concord and its environs. Thoreau's final stage was the never-ending falling apart and tarnishing of whatever humans build.

The Boulder Wall can help us mentally absorb the full sweep of deep time and explore Thoreau's appreciation of it in *Walden.*

### The thunking of stone on stone when building walls

"To what end, pray, is so much stone hammered? In Arcadia, when I was there, I did not see any hammering stone. Nations are possessed with an insane ambition to perpetuate the memory of themselves by the amount of hammered stone they leave. What if equal pains were taken to smooth and polish their manners? . . . More sensible is a rod of stone wall that bounds an honest man's field than a hundred-gated Thebes that has wandered farther from the true end of life."

At the Boulder Wall it's easy to imagine the thunk of stones being stacked on other stones by the laborers who built the wall. That sound was ubiquitous in rural New England during Thoreau's era. He built and repaired fieldstone walls as a common laborer. In contrast, he detested the cutting (hammering) of stone for vainglorious monuments.

We start with the planetary geology of earthly formation. Nearly five billion years ago, our planet was created within a universe nearly three times that age. That's when the truly primeval matter from which everything at Walden Pond was made: the nitrogen in the air Thoreau breathed, the oxygen in the $H_2O$ he drank, the carbon of the pine and oak woodland he lived beneath, the calcium in his bones, and the silicon of the stones he appreciated for their symbolism and utility.

Henry was fascinated by Earth's "mornings of creation." When near the summit of Maine's Mount Katahdin, and when standing on granite, he experienced a life-changing epiphany that stayed with him always.

This was that Earth of which we have heard, made out of Chaos and Old Night ... It was the fresh and natural surface of the planet Earth, as it was made forever and ever ... some star's surface, some hard matter in its home!

Thoreau then explored the tectonic geology of rock creation, which uses discrete minerals for raw materials. One of Earth's simplest minerals is graphite, composed of pure carbon and visible as tiny specks in some darker stones of the Boulder Wall. Graphite—known as *plumbago* or *black lead* during the nineteenth cen-tury—allowed the Thoreau family to live a middle-class life. With this mineral, mined from rock veins, they manufactured the pencils and powdered graphite that supported them financially during most of Henry's life.

### Pitch pine
#### (*Pinus rigida*)

"I used to resort to the northeast side of Walden, which the sun, reflected from the pitch pine woods and the stony shore, made the fireside of the pond; it is so much pleasanter and wholesomer to be warmed by the sun while you can be, than by an artificial fire."

Boulder Wall coincides with Thoreau's "fireside," Walden's warmest and driest corner, where pitch pine grew in abundance. Pitch pine is a small- to medium-sized tree, often with an irregular shape. It out-competes other pines on acidic dry soils, especially where woods have been burned off. The deep taproot of pitch pines allows them to thrive where more majestic pines cannot. A high resin content (pitch), especially in stumps, made pitch pine Thoreau's favorite fuel.

Unlike graphite, most minerals are combinations of elements. The pairing of silicon and oxygen makes familiar quartz. The pairing of hydrogen and oxygen makes ice. Like quartz, pond ice is a true mineral with a hexagonal structure, though the former has a much higher melting temperature, comparable to that of a blast furnace. Countless combinations of high-melting-point minerals—especially mica, quartz, pyroxene, garnet, amphibole, and various kinds of feldspar—created the silicate bedrock crust of New England.

Within the Boulder Wall we can see the variety of rock types that constitute New England: granite is massively grainy, gneiss is banded, schist is shiny with mica, quartzite is light-colored, and amphibolite is speckled black. All were created between 250 and 400 million years ago when the crust was squeezed, welded, and stretched within the roots of ancient mountain systems whose lofty peaks have long since vanished. A series of continental collisions had forced preexisting rock and sediment to descend more than ten miles downward, where they were pressurized, heated, sheared, and recrystallized. At such depths, this new rock deformed like warm taffy, creating folds, bulges, and compressions—features that can be easily seen in the Boulder Wall today.

Erosion has been relentless since the time of New England's main tectonic collisions. As the tall mountains were being removed, the deep warm crust supporting them from below rose upward at least ten vertical miles, cooled, and became a strong and brittle mass called *bedrock.*

As is true everywhere else on planet Earth, Walden Pond is underlain by such solid rock. Drill holes near the Visitor Center, rare outcrops in the surrounding hills, and geophysical surveys reveal that the rock below Walden Pond is weaker than elsewhere and is especially weak below its deepest hole.

The moving ice sheet picked up jagged blocks of bedrock. These blocks skittered southward like bumper cars being sheared above stationary rock. Large stones broke down into progressively smaller ones, making granules and sand in the process. Countless collisions crushed and rubbed the original sharp corners, creating billions of stones milled into lumpy shapes. These are the cobbles and boulders seen in the wall and on Walden's stony shore. Some are nearly round, some are jagged, and most are nondescript.

Within the hillside behind the wall are millions of large cobbles and small boulders just like the ones in the Boulder Wall. They were carried and dumped near Walden either directly by the ice sheet, or washed through meltwater tunnels. Accompanying the stones was a much more copious load of sand, the water-rinsed residue of glacially crushed stone. All of this material—jagged rock, lumpy stone, and sand of various textures—was deposited in the vicinity of Walden Pond by the last ice sheet.

Next came the human handling of the stones, in this case the anonymous workers who built our Boulder Wall. Thoreau did something similar when he built his house foundation, especially the part beneath his chimney. We won't be able to see the ruins of Thoreau's house foundation because some of the stone was recycled for a similar use elsewhere, and some was buried beneath the back-fill and soil of the House Site.

Let's imagine breaking the Boulder Wall apart, chipping away the mortar, and tossing the stones back to the water's

**Thomas B. Brennan supervised construction in 1957.**

The mortared Boulder Wall was built by an unknown masonry contractor (and folk artist) working for the Middlesex County Commissioners. In summer 1957, its chairman, Thomas B. Brennan, supervised an aggressive makeover of the shoreline. Creating and enlarging the swimming beaches required cutting the trees, excavating the banks back, and stabilizing the over-steepened slopes with retaining walls such as this one. That same summer, the Thoreau Society obtained a court injunction to halt the reengineering of the pond landscape, perceived as a desecration of Thoreau's legacy.

edge. That's where many of them came from, which is why Thoreau described the pond edge as "composed of a belt of smooth rounded white stones like paving stones." There, at the water's edge, glacial boulders and cobbles had been concentrated by waves from fifteen millennia of intermittent storms, pressed flat by the weight of the ice, smoothed by shoaling sand, and bleached by the sun.

Since Thoreau's time, however, the shore has become much less stony because thousands of its stones were harvested to create the memorial cairn and the twentieth-century architectural hardscape. Many more have been tossed into the water or out onto the ice for entertainment, a seemingly benign and almost irresistible pleasure. Given Walden's high visitation rates, a century of stone-throwing and stone-skidding is enough to denude the entire perimeter of what Thoreau considered a paved stony shore. The shore has become sandier as well, thanks to the accelerated bank erosion of the twentieth century.

The final process transforming the Boulder Wall is the natural weathering that's taken place since its construction. This includes the physical disintegration caused by heating and freezing; the chemical decomposition caused by mildly acid rainfall; and the biological surface roughening caused by lichens, bacteria, and moss. Collectively, these modern processes are darkening the stones with a patina, roughening their surfaces, and causing the mortar to fall apart.

Let's take a final look at the stone wall. In it, we're seeing visual stories spanning the eternity that Walden Pond symbolizes. Each wall is a library of earthen books. Each stone has a story to tell. Each mineral is a clue to the past. Each element is universal.

We touch the boulders one final time, turn to the west, and walk away. We're leaving our world of modernity and heading west into "Thoreau's World" of literary history. For the first time since our tour began, we'll be able to stretch our legs and walk at least five minutes without pausing. Our walk will carry us back in time.

## NORTHWEST: THOREAU'S WORLD

An old culvert, landscaping timbers, riprap boulders, and bank sediment lie jumbled together after bank collapse and shoreline erosion. The steep bank between the northeast and northwest sectors is heavily disturbed by human impact.

Today, traveling between "Our World" in the northeast sector and "Thoreau's World" in the northwest sector is as easy as walking a sidewalk. In Thoreau's day, however, this distance was an ankle-twisting barrier to pedestrian travel. Deadfall trees would have forced him to zigzag up and down the slope. Paths along the stony shore would have been blocked by trees leaning out over the water. Only during times of very low water would Henry have been able to walk this part of the pond shore. "Unlike many ponds," he wrote, "its shore is cleanest when the water

The eastern side of Thoreau's Cove at low water, with a southwesterly view over the bar at its mouth.

is lowest." Not once have I found a description of Thoreau walking this part of the bank.

Thoreau claimed he could see a trail in this vicinity, but only from the "middle of the pond in winter, just after a light snow has fallen, appearing as a clear undulating white line." This trail, "hardly distinguishable close at hand," was probably a former game trail created by animals that were locally extinct in Thoreau's time—for example, whitetail deer. The faintness of the trail in this vicinity would also have been due to its continuous erasure by soil creep, a natural process that is quite rapid on such steep slopes.

This part of the Pond Path was created beginning in 1931 using the age-old cut-and-fill technique. With saws and equipment, contractors working for the Middlesex County Commissioners excavated the bank on the uphill side, pushed that debris to the downhill side, and compacted it as best they could. After that they prayed that vegetation would stabilize the bank before it collapsed or was gullied. The result was a flat path with artificially steepened slopes on both sides.

Unfortunately, the original Pond Path collapsed in many places. Heavy foot traffic compacted the trail, preventing rain and snowmelt from soaking in. Heavy storms generated runoff as if on city streets. This triggered gullies in low spots, which triggered bank collapse. Given this vulnerability, we're lucky the trail works as well as it does.

After we walk a few more minutes westward, the woods will quickly brighten at the entrance to Thoreau's Cove. An open field of water looms ahead while the main part of the lake keeps to our left. At this point, the Pond Path intersects with a stone stairway descending the hill from the north on our right.

We are about to take the first of two short detours off the Pond Path. We'll climb that stone stairway to its junction with the Ridge Path, a boulder-studded trail that doubles back to the east. This trail will flatten with distance as we keep to the right and draw near its local crest. There, we'll find a steep overlook of the pond protected by a wire fence. We've reached the next stop.

## AT A GLANCE

**Object:** Bare Peak was Thoreau's name for the rounded summit nearest his house. Below the hilltop is a steep slope standing at the angle of repose, the natural slope for any granular material such as sand and gravel. This slope continues below the water.

**Location:** GPS coordinates 42° 26' 26.29" N, 71° 20' 25.94" W, 200 ft. The location is at the local crest of the Ridge Path near the wire fence overlooking the pond.

**Moment:** On April 24, 1918, photographer H. W. Gleason visited Bare Peak following a recent clear-cut of the trees. This ex-minister from Minnesota "discovered" Thoreau in 1895, moved east, and dedicated his life to photographing Thoreau's places.

The steep, straight, high slope below Bare Peak was a sheet of gravel, boulders, and sand before it was vegetated thousands of years ago. All of Walden's shore is surrounded by similar, though less spectacular, slopes that formed above growing kettles.

**Fun Fact:** The slope below Bare Peak likely inspired Thoreau's exaggerated claim that he could leap into the water to a depth over his head in a single bound.

**Nature:** When Thoreau stood on this peak on a calm day, he enjoyed watching the lake surface being enlivened by fish rising from below and insects descending from above.

# 5: BARE PEAK

## Sense of Place

*Thoreau's favorite overlook of the pond was from a summit only several minutes' walk from his house. This hilltop had been clear-cut of trees, allowing him to look down a straight, steep slope into the clear, aquamarine water of Walden's central basin.*

Reaching the local crest of the Ridge Path brings us to the highest overlook of our whole tour. Turning to the right, we look out through the trees and over the blue water toward the distant southern horizon. Remnants of the ancient delta plain are sometimes visible through the trees. Sixteen thousand years ago, we would have been looking out over a windswept gravel plain covered with gravel bars and turbid channels. Walden Pond did not yet exist.

Now let's walk over to the

### Henry's overlook of Walden's tallest steep slope

"The shore . . . is so steep that in many places a single leap will carry you into water over your head; and were it not for its remarkable transparency, that would be the last to be seen of its bottom till it rose on the opposite side. Some think it is bottomless."

The view looking down from Bare Peak into the water provides a fine example of Thoreau's greatly exaggerated description. The steep terrestrial slope continues beneath the water as a steep aquatic slope that extends another sixty feet down.

fence, lean over it slightly, and look down into the water that deepens rapidly near the shore. On a clear day, the water's spectral color

Common loon (*Gavia immer*). For Thoreau, this migrating species symbolized the wild. (Courtesy of the U.S. Fish & Wildlife Service)

changes from the bank outward, from clear to yellowish, to blue, and finally to green. Henry described the transition.

> Lying between the earth and the heavens, it [the pond] partakes of the color of both. Viewed from a hilltop it reflects the color of the sky; but near at hand it is of a yellowish tint next the shore where you can see the sand, then a light green, which gradually deepens to a uniform dark green in the body of the pond.

Why is green such a dominant color here? Let's start with pure sunlight, often called *white light*. When reflected to our eyes, we see every wavelength of the visible spectrum. This is why shallow water is transparent. None of the colors are absorbed. Instead, all are reflected. As water deepens, however, light must travel farther down into the water and back out again before reaching our eyes. Thus, more of the longer wavelengths are absorbed. The reds, oranges, and yellows are absorbed, leaving the greens and blues to scatter back. At greater depths, blue light and violet light are selectively absorbed by dissolved compounds, concentrating the scattering of green-blue and emerald green light back to our eyes. When Thoreau called Walden a "clear and deep green well," he was using its color as an index of clarity, which signaled purity. His friend Nathaniel Hawthorne thought Walden water was the "very purest liquid in the world."

At further depth, all of the light is absorbed and everything goes to black, even under the clearest conditions. At the blackout depth the light is said to be *extinct*. Scuba divers have taken video cameras down to Walden's depths to illustrate this effect. Ever so gradually they see a continuous parade of spectral color that begins clear and ends in abyssal blackness near the bottom.

## The common loon symbolized solitude and wildness.

"As I was paddling along the north shore one very calm October afternoon . . . a loon . . . sailing out from the shore toward the middle a few rods in front of me, set up his wild laugh and betrayed himself. I pursued with a paddle and he dived, but when he came up I was nearer than before. He dived again, but I miscalculated the direction he would take, and we were fifty rods apart when he came to the surface this time, for I had helped to widen the interval; and again he laughed long and loud, and with more reason than before . . . making the woods ring far and wide."

Perhaps the most famous animal story in *Walden* is of a loon flying over Bare Peak, landing on Walden Pond, and engaging Thoreau in a game of hide-and-seek. The excerpt above is from a much longer passage, an extended metaphor for the human search for wildness within ourselves and our proper place in nature. Interestingly, Thoreau used the archaic species name *Colymbus glacialis* (great northern diver) as a literary device to allude to ice-sheet glaciation from the north. In New England today, the preferred species name is *Gavia immer* (common loon). Loons are fast-swimming and deep-diving predators propelled by large webbed feet set far back on the body, making them clumsy walkers. Loons live mainly on small fish that they scan for and chase underwater. Being steep and stony, the Walden shore made terrible nesting habitat for loons. Nevertheless, these migratory birds came regularly to rest and feed on the pond.

Now let's sweep our eyes up from the water and to the left until we face east. We're now looking parallel to both the length of the lake and its tallest, straightest slope. Sweeping farther uphill to our left reveals the top of a local summit, which Thoreau aptly named "Bare Peak" because it was then bare of trees. He gave the name "Wooded Peak" to a higher, more distant summit on the same ridge since it had not yet been clear-cut. Thoreau enjoyed sunny Bare Peak not only for its view, but also because it provided perfect habitat for delicious huckleberries, a tart cousin of blueberries. When he exclaimed, "I am monarch of all I survey," he was proclaiming from such a lookout.

After Thoreau left the pond, the woods on the summit and hillside of Bare Peak re-grew and were re-cut in 1918. Since then, the forest has grown back. But the salient landform in this vicinity always remained clearly visible: the most dramatic slope of the Walden perimeter. During glacial retreat, this slope was a continuous sheet of boulders, cobbles, and pebbles standing at the angle of repose. Ever so gradually, the slope became covered by tundra that gathered in enough blowing dust to make a soil. Brush moved in, then trees, and finally the woods of "Thoreau's World." The granular materials beneath the soil no longer skitter, slide, roll, and bounce down

> ## The ringing of church bells from far away
>
> "Sometimes, on Sundays, I heard the bells, the Lincoln, Acton, Bedford, or Concord bell, when the wind was favorable, a faint, sweet, and, as it were, natural melody, worth importing into the wilderness. At a sufficient distance over the woods this sound acquires a certain vibratory hum, as if the pine needles in the horizon were the strings of a harp which it swept."
>
> Though Thoreau refused to attend church on Sundays, he loved the sound of church bells reaching out to him in Walden Woods from faraway towns. According to Thoreau, one of Concord's steeples was visible from Bare Peak.

the slope. Instead, they move slowly via a process called *soil creep.* Believe it or not, the thick, root-penetrated, moist soil is slowly creeping downhill like a rug being dragged by gravity over the underlying coarse gravel.

When heading up the Ridge Path to this stop, we passed many stones that were larger and less rounded than at previous stops. Their concentration reveals this ridge to be a *moraine,* from a French word for "mound of earth." To create this ridge, stony glacial sediment tumbled directly from the ice. The resulting moraine is higher, coarser, and more irregular than the flat delta plain forming at the same time.

Thoreau recognized that this ridge was stonier than his shrub oak plateau and realized it was the source of the stones that lined the Walden shore in his day: "I observe that the surrounding hills are remarkably full of the same kind of stones . . . and,

The boulders below Bare Peak often have jagged edges because they were released directly from the glacial margin, instead of being rolled in meltwater tunnels.

moreover, there are most stones where the shore is most abrupt." Here, he is specifically referring to Bare Peak and the collapse slope below it, which is what we're looking at now.

Just north of where we're standing is a small, elongated, leafy, closed depression roughly parallel to the trail and about fifty feet to the north. It's clearly visible in the shaded-relief topographic image on page 27. Like Walden Pond, this small, leafy basin is also a kettle. But in this case, it's a dry kettle hole because it didn't sink low enough to reach the groundwater table.

We now turn around 180 degrees to look southward over Walden's big-

### White oak
#### (*Quercus alba*)

"He [the woodchopper] has a great bundle of white oak bark under his arm for a sick man, gathered this Sunday morning."

The white oak, which Thoreau called the "king of trees," is a large, muscular, beautiful hardwood that was greatly prized for lumber, especially by shipwrights. White oak prefers warm, dry, sunny, elevated soils such as the extensive slope of Bare Peak. Though Thoreau loved the tree, he doesn't describe a single white oak in *Walden*. The species may have been locally absent, owing to the generally sterile soils of the Walden perimeter and to generations of cutting.

gest and deepest western basin. There, and only there, meltdown occurred in two stages. The initial subsidence gave rise to the coves of Walden Pond and to the many irregular hollows, ridges, and kettles over much of Walden Woods. Later meltdown subsidence was dramatic above what is now the pond's deepest, darkest, quietest basin. There, the top of the ancient delta plain sank straight down to a depth of about 170 feet, easily enough to submerge a fifteen-story building. The depth was due to the great thickness of stagnant ice at a point where the ancestral bedrock valley had been deepest because the rock had been weakest.

## J. Walter Goldthwait mapped the geology in 1905.

The pioneering geologist James Walter Goldthwait was the first scientist (after Thoreau) to work out the origin of Walden Pond. He mapped the glacial geology of the Concord River Valley as part of his graduate work at Harvard University. Goldthwait received a Ph.D. in Cambridge in 1906, the same year Thoreau's *Journal* was published in Boston by Houghton Mifflin Company. One year earlier, in 1905, Goldthwait published "The Sand Plains of Glacial Lake Sudbury" in the *Bulletin of the Museum of Comparative Zoology at Harvard College.* One of the sand plains Goldthwait identified was the vast plain of sand and gravel that had sunk downward to create Walden Pond. He would have seen the ancient surface best from Bare Peak.

To return to the Pond Path, we must retrace our steps back down the Ridge Path, and then back down the stone stairway we climbed. At that point we'll head west on the Pond Path for another twenty feet or so until the trail takes a hard right turn to the north. If the water is low enough, we'll be able to see the sandbar fronting Thoreau's Cove. Our next stop is wherever we can see through the trees and over the cove.

## AT A GLANCE

**Object:** Thoreau's Cove is the nearest part of Walden Pond to Thoreau's original House Site. As with the other three coves, it's fairly shallow, has a bar at the mouth, is distinct from the main part of the lake, and was created in a roughly triangular shape.

**Location:** GPS coordinates 42° 26' 27.26" N, 71° 20' 29.72" W, 161 ft. After we turn the corner of the Pond Path to the north, we'll take the first viewpoint across Thoreau's Cove to the west.

**Moment:** In September 1902, plans were made to deforest the land just north of the cove, create a large slaughterhouse for beef, and feed hundreds of hogs from the offal. These plans were rejected after national attention in the *New-York Tribune* and indignation from local residents.

The view across Thoreau's Cove from the opposite, western side at Stop 10, the Waterfront. Two people on the beach provide scale for the cove and its sandbar.

**Fun Fact:** West and north of Thoreau's Cove, groundwater flows away from the pond, so Thoreau's domestic activities would not have polluted Walden Pond.

**Nature:** When lying on the ice and studying the cove bottom, Thoreau observed the furrows, or trackways, made by the larvae of caddisflies. They resembled miniature versions of those made by clams in fine sand.

# 6: THOREAU'S COVE

## Sense of Place

*Thoreau's Cove is the first of four originally shallow and triangular-shaped coves that we will explore on our trip around Walden's western basin. Ralph Waldo Emerson bought the land above the cove in 1844 and gave Thoreau permission to live there.*

Turning the corner from the steep slope below Bare Peak into Thoreau's Cove elicits an almost magical feeling. Suddenly, the scale of the water view shrinks by an order of magnitude, and the surface becomes more tranquil. Turning this corner also puts all of the twentieth-century shoreline improvements out of sight behind the Bare Peak moraine. Very few of the swimming hordes of the Eastern Shore make it this far.

Throughout the nineteenth century, a carriage path connected Thoreau's Cove to Walden Street along the edge of the Wyman Lot. This route, the so-called Wyman

### Henry's cove definition

"Of five coves, three, or all which had been sounded, were observed to have a bar quite across their mouths and deeper water within, so that the bay tended to be an expansion of water within the land not only horizontally but vertically, and to form a basin or independent pond."

For Thoreau, true coves are shallow extensions of the lake, not merely bays in a steep shore. Thoreau's Cove was his archetype for how they should look. None were named in his day. This guide uses three other cove names: Ice Fort Cove, Sandbank Cove, and Deep Cove.

Road, was the shortest distance for visitors coming from Concord Center and Emerson's parlor. Additionally, this path had the advantage of accessing the pond via a gentle incline, in contrast to the steep slope below the pond's eastern rim. For these two reasons, Thoreau's Cove became the main destination for town residents during the late 1830s and early 1840s. It's no accident that Thoreau chose to live directly on the main thoroughfare for the amblers and dreamers of the transcendental era. Following his departure, the Wyman Road continued to provide easy access to the shore of the cove (that now bears his name) well into the twentieth century.

Thoreau's first remembered visit to the cove happened in 1824, long before Emerson moved to Concord. Henry was a seven-year-old boy being brought to the pond by his family via this easy route. The outing would have included his father, John; mother, Cynthia; older brother, John Jr.; older sister, Helen; and little sister, Sophia. Henry remembered seeing a "narrow sand-bar running into it, with very deep water on one side." On that bar he helped his family "boil a kettle of chowder, some six rods

## Yellow perch— common, but beautiful in schools

"The water is so transparent that the bottom can easily be discerned at the depth of twenty-five or thirty feet. Paddling over it, you may see, many feet beneath the surface, the schools of perch and shiners, perhaps only an inch long, yet the former easily distinguished by their transverse bars, and you think that they must be ascetic fish that find a subsistence there."

The shallow, clear water of Thoreau's Cove brought in schools of yellow perch (*Perca flavescens*) close to shore, where Thoreau enjoyed watching them. The yellow perch is actually more of a tarnished brass color than yellow. It is easily identified by its zebralike black transverse bars that help camouflage it from predators. Living mainly on zooplankton and small invertebrates, the yellow perch is a critical prey resource for predators in the water (pickerel and bass), in the air (ospreys and kingfishers), and on the shore (foxes and cats).

from the main shore," or about a hundred feet out.

During repeated later visits, he noted that the bar was "usually submerged," and walk-

Yellow perch (*Perca flavescens*). Schools of yellow perch accompanied Thoreau when he boated. (Duane Raver, courtesy of the U.S. Fish & Wildlife Service)

ing that far out had not "been possible to do for twenty-five years." Based on my own three decades of experience, the bar has also usually been submerged. But during the spring of 2017, that same sandy bar extended more than 200 feet into the lake. Such exposure is a sure sign of a prolonged drought, which Concord had experienced the previous year.

The sandbar at the mouth of Thoreau's Cove is the largest and most conspicuous of the three bars Thoreau would later measure during his famous pond survey of 1846. Being quite gravelly today, the bar lies immediately downwind of the tallest slope (Bare Peak) in a setting where strong easterly storm winds shape bank sediment into a west-propagating bar.

Thoreau's Cove is the best place for us to reflect on Thoreau's genius, not as a writer, but as a curiosity-driven, keenly observant, quantitative field scientist who wouldn't let go of a question until he had an answer. As an offshoot of his famous pond survey, Henry worked out a mathematical rule to define coves and linked them to the underlying bedrock structure. His achievement is amazing, especially given that his reasons for going to Walden were personal and philosophical—not scientific.

First, Henry combined his recognition of the normally submerged bar at Thoreau's Cove with his survey measurements of cove length, breadth, and depth. He then proposed a geometrical formula for true coves to differentiate them from mere bays in the shore.

> In proportion as the mouth of the cove was wider compared with its length, the water over the bar was deeper compared with that in the basin. Given, then, the length and breadth of the cove, and the character of the surrounding shore, and you have almost elements enough to make out a formula for all cases.

Second, he used his formula to confirm that coves had a common origin different from the common origin of the three deep basins.

Of five coves, three, or all which had been sounded, were observed to have a bar quite across their mouths and deeper water within, so

The sandbar at the mouth of Thoreau's Cove, looking east to the boathouse, on April 8, 2017. In Thoreau's time, this bar was usually submerged.

that the bay tended to be an expansion of water within the land not only horizontally but vertically, and to form a basin or independent pond.

Finally, he noticed that the coves were aligned with nearby hills and ridges, which, in turn, follow the underlying rock structure.

The regularity of the bottom [of the western basin] and its conformity to the shores and the range of the neighboring hills were so perfect that a distant promontory betrayed itself in the soundings quite across the pond . . . Cape becomes bar, and plain shoal, and valley and gorge deep water and channel.

Being shallow, Thoreau's Cove lies entirely within the summer-warmed, wind-mixed upper layer of Walden Pond, typically twenty feet thick. This upper layer "floats" on the colder, denser water lying motionless within the pond's three deep basins. Lake scientists—called *limnologists*—refer to this upper layer as the *epilimnion* and to the lower mass as the *hypolimnion*. During the summer, the whole upper layer warms to a temperature in the high 70s Fahrenheit. The water was plenty warm for Thoreau's twice-daily swims or "baths," but too warm to drink. For summer plumbing, Henry used his boat, a cord, and a bucket to haul cold water up from below and kept it cool in his cellar. His alternative was to visit nearby springs, the coldest of which was Boiling Spring, named for the boiling bubbles of fine sand caused by artesian flow.

Below about thirty feet, the water is too deep to be sun-warmed and wind-mixed, so it rests motionless for most of the year. Luckily, Walden's deep and shallow layers mix twice per year. During early winter, the surface water cools to 39 degrees Fahrenheit. At that temperature the surface water becomes heavier than the bottom water and plunges downward, pushing the slightly less dense bot-

## Huckleberry
### (*Gaylussacia baccata*)

"It is a vulgar error to suppose that you have tasted huckleberries who never plucked them. A huckleberry never reaches Boston; they have not been known there since they grew on her three hills. The ambrosial and essential part of the fruit is lost with the bloom which is rubbed off in the market cart, and they become mere provender."

The north shore of Thoreau's Cove had been clear-cut of its trees several times before Thoreau's sojourn to Walden Pond. This created the disturbed, dry, acidic, sunny conditions in which huckleberries thrive. This species is closely related to, and often included with, the more well-known highbush blueberry but is darker and more purple. When ripe, a huckleberry's fruit is less sweet, more tart, and more exotic than blueberries, accounting for Thoreau's passage above.

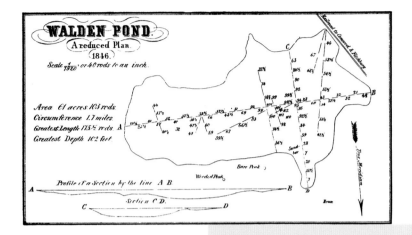

Thoreau's survey map of Walden Pond as published in *Walden* at ¼ scale. His profile A–B shows all three of Walden's large basins (eastern, central, and western) and the smaller depression of Ice Fort Cove. (Courtesy of the Walden Woods Project)

tom water upward. This cycle continues for a few days until the whole pond is mixed, and the water reaches the same uniformly cold temperature throughout. Something similar happens during early spring, when the icy surface water plunges down into slightly less dense bottom water. On March 6, 1846, Henry measured a thirty-degree difference between warm surface and cold bottom water. His description of this process of water-layering, called *stratification,* was a pioneering observation.

Henry loved lying on the thin ice of Thoreau's Cove and peering at the bottom. For most of the year, the view of the bottom is distorted by ripples and waves moving over the surface of the water. But during freeze-up, the water is covered by a thin layer of ice that resembles a transparent sheet of plate glass. Such ice is literally a window to another world.

Unlike the shore of Thoreau's Cove, the shore elsewhere has been dramatically altered. Here at Ice Fort Cove, stones were hauled in to reduce bank erosion and stabilize the trail.

The first ice is especially interesting and perfect, being hard, dark, and transparent, and affords the best opportunity that ever offers for examining the bottom where it is shallow; for you can lie at your length on ice only an inch thick, . . . and study the bottom at your leisure, only two or three inches distant, like a picture behind a glass, and the water is necessarily always smooth then.

Somewhere along the straight eastern edge of Thoreau's Cove, we'll find a place to look through the trees to the opposite shore. There we will see a shoreline prominence of golden brown gravel that Thoreau called his "pond-side." We will call it his Waterfront, a stop we will visit four stops ahead.

Farther north we will see the tip of Thoreau's Cove (see photo on page 240). Though closest to his House Site, this part of Walden Pond is very shallow and protected from the wind. In place of sloshing waves on a stony shore, we can find mud, pollen, mashed-up leaves, twigs, the occasional dead fish, and other types of flotsam. Left on the shore by receding water levels, this organic matter decomposes in place, venting a sulfurous odor. Occasionally, a sudsy gray foam will develop from this organic brew.

> ## Carl T. Ramsey went skinny-dipping in 1912.
>
> Ramsey was a literary pilgrim to Walden Pond in search of Thoreau's legacy. In August 1912, he went skinny-dipping in Thoreau's Cove. In so doing, he ignored and flaunted the posted signs that "suitable clothing" must be worn. The following year, he described the experience in his book *A Pilgrimage to the Haunts of Thoreau.* "How it thrills me! I give a wild yell . . . I am regenerated. I lave my sins in the water of Walden!" Here, Ramsey was following Thoreau's example of swimming naked as a "religious exercise."

We're done with the east side of Thoreau's Cove. As we continue northward along the Pond Path, we'll eventually step up to a small wooden bridge. Looking left, or west, from the midpoint of the bridge will give us a view of Thoreau's Cove. Looking right, or east, is the view for our next stop.

## AT A GLANCE

*Object:* The meadow lies within Walden Pond's fourth kettle basin, its ecologically richest. The meadow toggles back and forth between being a round grassy plain and a shallow part of the lake.

*Location:* GPS coordinates 42° 26' 29.74" N, 71° 20' 30.22" W, 161 ft. The coordinates are at the center of the bridge overlooking the meadow to the east. On the map, however, the stop appears at the center of the meadow to show the place of interest. Park rules prohibit walking in the meadow.

*Moment:* On Christmas Eve, 1841, three years before Ralph Waldo Emerson bought the Wyman Lot, Thoreau wrote: "I want to go soon and live away by the pond where I shall hear only the wind whispering among the reeds." Many scholars link this statement to tranquil Wyman Meadow, even though reeds are limited and the wind is usually slight.

An easterly view across Wyman Meadow in May 2017 shows the basin that is sometimes part of Walden Pond. Ecologically, this is the richest part of Walden's shore.

*Fun Fact:* Wyman Meadow is classified as a deep marsh and designated as a certified vernal pool by the state of Massachusetts. It's great habitat for frogs and salamanders.

*Nature:* In 1847, when living at Walden, Thoreau collected fish from this meadow and the adjacent lake and sent them to the Swiss-born scientist Louis Agassiz, who was building a reference collection of dead animals at Harvard College.

# 7: WYMAN MEADOW

## Sense of Place

*Wyman Meadow is by far the ecologically richest part of our tour. This small kettle is most often a grassy meadow, but it becomes part of the larger lake when the groundwater table rises. Thoreau enjoyed boating over this meadow when it was flooded.*

ooking east from the bridge will probably give us a view that Thoreau saw quite often: a grassy hollow that was lush green in the growing season, mottled brown-white in winter, and honey colored in fall and spring. "Rattlesnake grass" was the term he used for the vegetation during drought. Sometimes he saw a wet marsh surrounded by rushes and covered by floating aquatic plants, such as lily pads.

But the times that fascinated

### Henry's transient bay

"The pond rises and falls, but whether regularly or not, and within what period, nobody knows, though, as usual, many pretend to know . . . the pond has risen steadily for two years, and now, in the summer of '52, is just five feet higher than when I lived there, or as high as it was thirty years ago, and fishing goes on again in the meadow."

Thoreau watched the water flood and recede from Wyman Meadow in response to changes in the height of the lake. This variability between wet and dry conditions creates ecological richness.

Henry the most were when he saw the meadow flooded deeply with rippling blue water to become a key-shaped bay of the lake. When

The Guide to Walden Pond

## The horned pout symbolized primitiveness.

"Sometimes, after staying in a village parlor till the family had all retired, I have returned to the woods, and, partly with a view to the next day's dinner, spent the hours of midnight fishing from a boat by moonlight, serenaded by owls and foxes, and hearing, from time to time, the creaking note of some unknown bird close at hand. These experiences were very memorable and valuable to me—anchored in forty feet of water, and twenty or thirty rods from the shore, surrounded sometimes by thousands of small perch and shiners, dimpling the surface with their tails in the moonlight . . . At length you slowly raise, pulling hand over hand, some horned pout squeaking and squirming to the upper air."

The horned pout was a common nineteenth-century name for the brown bullhead (*Ameiurus nebulosus*), a species of catfish. Thoreau enjoyed watching them breed in the shallower, warmer, muddier water of Wyman Meadow. Pouts are frequently mentioned in *Walden*, likely because of their abundance. The weak light and sludgy bottoms of Walden's deep basins provided protection against predators as well as good food opportunities for these bottom feeders. This fish was likely introduced into Walden Pond, because catfish aren't usually abundant in such pure waters.

this happened, Henry would launch his boat from the other side of Thoreau's Cove, row through a narrow passage where the bridge stands today, and go fishing in this isolated basin. "I was accustomed to fish from a boat in a secluded cove in the woods" in a place "long since converted into a meadow." Henry didn't fish alone. When flooded, Wyman Meadow offered the best fishing at the pond. This situation also gave Thoreau a waterfront view close to his house.

Over the years, I've seen Wyman Meadow in all three of its basic modes: deeply flooded, shallow pond, and grassy meadow. When deeply flooded, the meadow becomes just another part of the lake with no detectable current at the narrows between it and Thoreau's Cove. At such times, Wyman Meadow became an important fish nursery for the whole lake, and in Thoreau's era held schools of fingerling perch, pickerel, sunfish, minnows, and bullheads, which he

–106–

called "pout." On several occasions I've seen a shallow pond with lily pads and reeds. Most of the time, however, Wyman Meadow has been a rich grassy meadow that seems strangely out of place next to the otherwise stony-sandy perimeter, where hardly a weed can be found.

Before a bridge was built in response to the high water of 2010, the boundary between Wyman Meadow and Thoreau's Cove was usually a narrow, weedy sandbar. Thoreau ambled over something similar to and from Bare Peak. If shallowly flooded, he crossed on what he called a "stick" bridge, probably a tree branch tossed across the isthmus. During my three decades of intermittently visiting Wyman Meadow, only once have I seen water trickle westward over this bar. The singularity and trivial magnitude of this surface flow showcases an obvious truth: that Walden Pond is overwhelmingly dominated by groundwater flow moving from east to west.

The condition of Wyman Meadow during any given week is determined entirely by the height of standing water in Thoreau's Cove, to which it drains. In turn, the flood and drought "stages" of the cove is driven entirely by the elevation of the water table in the adjacent aquifer.

"The pond rises and falls," Thoreau wrote, "but whether regularly or not, and within what period, nobody knows, though, as usual, many pretend to know." In this *Walden* passage Thoreau assigns these variations a sense of mystery and cautions his readers to avoid jumping to conclusions. He knew that pond stage was the sum of multiple groundwater responses. "It is commonly higher in the winter and lower in the summer, though not corresponding to the general wet and dryness." Thoreau was so interested in this phenomenon that he measured it regularly over the span of several decades, longer than any other feature at the pond. One of his hundreds of measurements of pond stage—April 27, 1854—was the last item of information to enter *Walden* before it was published. This physical

The rise and fall of Walden's shore is indicated by lines of debris (strand-lines) at Ice Fort Cove, where easterly winds blow across the full length of the lake.

measurement was transferred from a scribble on an envelope to the publisher's page proofs, bypassing the submitted manuscript and editorial process completely.

A recent mathematical modeling study found that a single factor accounts for much of Walden's up-and-down variation. Data collected by the U.S. Geological Survey over a fifty-eight-year period show that the stage of Walden Pond most closely correlates with the average total precipitation for the preceding two years. Differences in heat-related evaporation and in the patterns of precipitation—rain versus snow, winter versus summer—have little effect. Apparently, it takes about two years for the average mass of the precipitation to flow sideways into the lake. Superimposed on this long-term trend is an annual cycle, which Thoreau recognized as beginning with a rapid rise due to snowmelt, a slow decline until leaf fall, a slight rise until freeze-up, and then a slow decline until the next snowmelt.

When drained, Wyman Meadow resembles dozens of kettle holes dotting Walden Woods to the north. This small basin helps us understand what an archetype glacial kettle looks like because it's small enough to be seen as one thing. The meadow's circular edge reveals the ideal bowl shape of a meltdown collapse. Above the lens of moist peaty soils are banks of dry gravel that are gracefully curved from top to bottom. Thus, Wyman Meadow offers a standard to which we can compare Walden's three larger basins. All have a shape similar to that of Wyman Meadow, but their enormous size and complete submergence make it hard to visualize their formation.

Ecologists classify Wyman Meadow as a *deep marsh* resembling those of the rich moist bottomlands of the Concord River Valley. Thoreau also called it a marsh: "a mink steals out of the marsh before my door and seizes a frog by the shore." Ecologists certify this marsh as a *vernal* pool, giving it special protection under town, state, and federal laws. Vernal pools are common in the small kettles of Walden Woods north of the lake, where water becomes

## Croaking frogs concentrated in Wyman Meadow.

"[T]hough there are almost no weeds [on Walden's shore], there are frogs there—who would fain keep up the hilarious rules of their old festal tables, though their voices have waxed hoarse and solemnly grave, mocking at mirth, . . . *tr-r-r-oonk, tr-r-r—oonk, tr-r-r-oonk!* and straightway comes over the water from some distant cove the same password repeated, where the next in seniority and girth has gulped down to his mark; and when this observance has made the circuit of the shores, then ejaculates the master of ceremonies, with satisfaction, *tr-r-r-oonk!*"

Wyman Meadow was an important breeding ground for the frogs of Walden Pond. This marsh was close enough to his House Site for him to hear frog noises.

seasonally trapped above local impermeable layers. Other small kettles in this vicinity are true kettle holes, being consistently dry. Instead of holding water, they hold cold, dense air. Thoreau greatly enjoyed walking into and out of these cool air pockets, which he called "refrigerators." There, the frost would arrive first and linger longest, and rare bog plants could be found.

The biological richness of Wyman Meadow offers us an opportunity to reflect on the limited biodiversity near the Pond Path. Walden's upland slopes and terraces are dry, open woodlands dominated by pine and oak with some hickory and other trees interspersed. The understory is a mix of tree seedlings, perennial brush, and herbaceous plants. Native and invasive shrubs and flowers fight for space. Walden's gravel shore follows a similar pattern around the whole perimeter, with headlands (prominences) being coarser and steeper, and the coves (recesses) being shallower and sandier. Walden's aquatic zone is also fairly similar everywhere (away from artificial beaches), with variations associated with water depth, wave power, and access to sunlight. One sentence from *Walden* captures all three zones—terrestrial, shoreline, aquatic—of the local ecosystem: "The perch swallows the grub-worm, the pickerel swallows the perch, and the fisherman swallows the pickerel; and so all the chinks in the scale of being are filled."

Generally, the vegetation near the Pond Path is a surprisingly uniform spontaneous (weedy) regrowth of woodland. The trees were either cut down or burned at least once prior to establishment of the park in 1922. Nevertheless, according to park ecologists, the modern vegetation is similar to "the hard and soft wood mix of Thoreau's day and includes mostly berry bushes, sumac, pitch pine, hickory and oak." Within this ecological uniformity exists local variety. Extra sunny and boulder-studded south-facing slopes support pitch pine. Windblown loamy soils of Thoreau's Bean Field remain fertile enough for agriculture. Deeply shaded portions of Walden's south shore support local stands of hemlock, with patches of moss on north-facing excavations. Much of today's local ecological variation results from patchy historic activities such as commercial wood harvesting and accidental fires set by flying railroad cinders.

The general uniformity of this terrestrial ecosystem near the Pond Path would quickly disappear if we extended our tour outward only one mile. Elsewhere in the park, Emerson's Cliff would offer the lichen-dominated flora of a dry, rocky habitat. The broader habitat of Walden Woods would take in the frost pockets to the north and offer us carnivorous bog plants. The eco-region of the Concord River Valley, notably Fairhaven Bay on the Sudbury River, would offer water lilies rooted in black muck.

## Highbush blueberry
### (*Vaccinium corymbosum*)

"[During times of high water] I have known the high blueberry bushes about the shore, which commonly produce no fruit, bear an abundant crop under these circumstances."

The highbush blueberry thrives in the full sun and moist soils such as those along the edge of Wyman Meadow. This shrub, with its pinnate leaves and large blue berries, grows in dense thickets on acid soils. The species favors recently cut or burned woodland. Formerly an important Native American food source, highbush blueberries have become an important agricultural crop.

Based on a survey published in 2013 by the Massachusetts Department of Conservation and Recreation, there are 145 species of plants within Walden Pond State Reservation. We will see many of these plants on our pond tour, though we will not pause to identify any particulars. Detailed species lists are publicly available. Twelve of these species are terrestrial invasive plants of special concern,

**Tommy Wyman died a debtor in 1843.**

Wyman Meadow is named for John Wyman, who, before the American Revolution, squatted in a small house on Walden Road above the eastern bank of Walden Pond. Wyman was a potter who made earthenware crockery there in the middle of the eighteenth century. John Wyman's younger relative, Thomas, would later buy and farm an adjacent parcel of land that became known as the Wyman Lot. In September 1844 Tommy's lot was auctioned off to pay his creditors. Ralph Waldo Emerson was the only bidder.

four of which are well known and fairly ubiquitous: Asiatic bittersweet, Japanese barberry, multiflora rose, and Japanese knotweed. These invasive plants are common near multiple stops. No federally or state-listed rare or endangered wildlife species are known to exist in the woodlands of our tour.

The woods of the Pond Path provide habitat for a variety of common mammals, reptiles, amphibians, and birds. Twenty-three species of mammals have been confirmed in the vicin-ity. Various species of mice, shrews, squirrels, and the weasel fam-ily are most common. Larger mammals include white-tailed deer, beavers, coyotes, foxes, raccoons, and fishers. The first three—deer, beaver, coyote—were locally extinct during Thoreau's time. Six spe-cies of reptiles have been identified, mainly turtles and snakes near the shore. Ten species of amphibians are confirmed. Although sala-manders, toads, and wood frogs are widely dispersed, they gather to breed in vernal pools, most importantly Wyman Meadow. True frogs are generally restricted to the pond shore. They are abundant when the water is high, and more rare when the water is low.

Bird watching is a popular activity at the park and in nearby towns. Based on the park's 2013 management plan, fifty-two species of birds have been sighted on the state reservation, with an addi-tional thirty sighted in nearby habitats, especially along the river. Some birds live locally year-round, some are seasonal residents, and some migrate through in a matter of days. The scarlet tanager,

Students on school trips commonly walk the Pond Path toward Thoreau's House Site. On the way, they cross the bridge to see Wyman Meadow, shown here in the background below the trees.

Baltimore oriole, swamp sparrow, spotted sandpiper, and belted kingfisher are especially popular with bird watchers.

The aquatic fauna and flora are mainly invisible—either submerged or microscopic. Two species of aquatic plants, however, are worth noting. Thoreau described the first as a "bright green weed . . . brought up on anchors even in mid-winter." His observation was of a leafy algae called *Nitella* that flourishes everywhere beneath the pond in a zone between twenty and forty feet deep. This algae is highly beneficial because it sops up excess nutrient and returns oxygen to the water, both of which help keep the water clear. The second species of note is the Acadian quillwort (*Isoetes acadiensis*), a primitive spore-bearing plant, and the only state-listed rare and endangered species anywhere near our tour. Though there are no known permanent populations of invasive aquatic plants, Eurasian water-milfoil (*Myriophyllum spicatum*) remains a persistent threat.

Thoreau noted that "this pond is not very fertile in fish" when compared to the nearby rivers, or even to Flint's Pond, which isn't a kettle lake. In *Walden,* he offered this inventory:

> There have been caught in Walden pickerel, one weighing seven pounds—to say nothing of another which carried off a reel with great velocity, which the fisherman safely set down at eight pounds because he did not see him—perch and pouts, some of each weighing over two pounds, shiners, chivins or roach (*Leuciscus pulchellus*), a very few breams, and a couple of eels, one weighing four pounds.

The modern fish inventory does not relate to Thoreau's inventory because the individual species have been actively managed since 1905. Aggressive manipulation of Walden's fish culminated in 1968 when all of the fish were poisoned in order to restock the pond with "favorable species," some of which Thoreau never encountered.

Currently, the Massachusetts Department of Fish and Game stocks three species of trout (rainbow, brook, and brown) and two species of bass (smallmouth and largemouth). Persistent populations that Thoreau noticed include chain pickerel, yellow perch, brown bullhead, and sunfish (bluegill and pumpkinseed) that he called "bream." Consumption of fish from the pond is discouraged, owing to airborne mercury pollution from distant sources.

Our view of Wyman Meadow now ends at the center of the bridge. Let's continue across the northern half of the bridge and step down to the trail. As we begin walking up the hill, we'll probably see some erosion of the trail caused by surface runoff. This exposes small patches of reddish-brown rusty sand with the texture of granulated sugar. If visible, this well-sorted fine sand will be our best look at the sediment constituting the bulk of the aquifer that feeds Walden Pond.

If we continue for approximately 100 feet, we should see a sign to the left that says "House Site," with an arrow pointing the way. The trail will bring us to the place where Thoreau lived. As we approach, we'll see some granite posts to the right and a pile of stones to the left. We've arrived at our next stop.

## AT A GLANCE

**Object:** Thoreau's House Site is a cluster of features, notably the footprint of his former house (marked by granite posts), the memorial cairn of stones, the distant water view, and the intersection of three trails.

This southward view toward Walden Pond is over the former site of Thoreau's house, marked by granite posts. The memorial cairn, a mound of stones, is to the right.

**Location:** GPS coordinates 42° 26' 31.23" N, 71° 20' 33.20" W, 184 ft. This site is clearly identified by signage and is well-marked on the trail.

**Moment:** On August 1, 1846, Henry cohosted the annual meeting of the Concord Female Anti-Slavery Society at the House Site. This organization included his sisters, Helen and Sophia, and his mother, Cynthia. They endorsed "disunion," meaning the secession of the North from the slave-holding South to prevent civil war. Speaking at the meeting was Lewis Hayden, a fugitive slave from Kentucky.

**Fun Fact:** On July 4, 1845, Henry moved into his house before it was shingled, plastered, and bricked for a fireplace. Sunlight, breezes, and insects easily passed through the board walls nailed to the timbers. When inside, he compared himself to a bird in a cage.

**Nature:** Thoreau happily shared his home with various woodland creatures. He had "squirrels on the roof and under the floor, a whip-poor-will on the ridge-pole, a blue jay screaming beneath the window, [and] a hare or woodchuck under the house."

# 8: HOUSE SITE

## Sense of Place

*The House Site is the epicenter of "Thoreau's World" and a shrine to America's environmental consciousness. The house footprint and the memorial cairn create an unlikely pair of objects, one stable below the ground, the other changeable on the surface.*

The House Site is where Thoreau wrote the first draft of *Walden; or, Life in the Woods,* America's most famous book about place. On most mornings he sat at his small, green desk, dipped his pen into ink, and wrote on loose-leaf manuscript sheets as if possessed. On most nights, he was there as well. On most afternoons and evenings, however, he left his house, perhaps walking down the railroad tracks to take meals with his family, strolling over Wyman Road to the village center, wandering over woodland trails, or boating up and down his three rivers.

### Henry's woodsy yard

"My house was on the side of a hill, immediately on the edge of the larger wood, in the midst of a young forest of pitch pines and hickories, and half a dozen rods from the pond, to which a narrow footpath led down the hill. In my front yard grew the strawberry, blackberry, and life-everlasting, johnswort and goldenrod, shrub-oaks and sand-cherry, blueberry and groundnut."

Thoreau's House Site was just below the edge of a small hollow located within the larger hollow containing Walden Pond. The view from his western window, below which he kept his desk, overlooked a "yard" of brush that was regrowing from a recent clear-cut.

## The snowshoe hare was more easily heard than seen.

"The hares (*Lepus Americanus*) were very familiar. One had her form under my house all winter, separated from me only by the flooring, and she startled me each morning by her hasty departure when I began to stir—thump, thump, thump, striking her head against the floor timbers in her hurry. They used to come round my door at dusk to nibble the potato parings which I had thrown out, and were so nearly the color of the ground that they could hardly be distinguished when still. Sometimes in the twilight I alternately lost and recovered sight of one sitting motionless under my window."

Thoreau's House Site was colonized by all sorts of creatures who happily shared that space with him. In this passage, he describes the most common hare of his woods by its proper taxonomic name (*Lepus americanus*). The nickname *snowshoe* comes from the large size of this rabbit's hind feet. This species is also called the varying hare because its coat changes from dappled tawny brown in summer to white in winter. Mainly herbivorous, the snowshoe hare lives on grass, ferns, leaves, twigs, and bark. A snowshoe hare is mainly nocturnal and does not migrate or hibernate. Its predators are owls, foxes, hawks, and humans.

What we see now is not what Thoreau saw then. The woods of *Walden*'s subtitle were thinner and patchier, having been cut for fuel for many generations. The woods of today are taller and more continuous because fuel wood became less valuable in an age of fossil fuels. Hardly any wood harvesting has taken place since 1922, when this private land, fourteen acres known as the "Wyman Lot," was donated to the Commonwealth to help establish Walden Pond State Reservation.

The House Site, a quarter acre of mature woodland, is a holy shrine to Thoreau aficionados. "Mecca" was the word Walter Harding used to describe this place when he organized the first annual meeting of the Thoreau Society. Though the attendees planned to meet here at exactly 10:00 AM on the morning of July 12, 1941, imminent rainstorms kept them in town. Otherwise they would have walked fifteen minutes to reach the exact spot where Henry lived between July 4, 1845, and September 6, 1847.

Harding's invitation list was based on a mimeographed newsletter compiled by Raymond Adams, Harding's graduate advisor. This pair of literary scholars, one a mentor and one a protégé, conducted a short ceremony for nearly two hundred people before adjourning for lunch at the Colonial Inn, a continuing landmark of Concord tourism. Henry had lived there as an infant, in a house later incorporated into the inn. The building was then a boarding house run by Henry's aunts, and owned by Henry's paternal grandfather, Jean Thoreau, a seafaring merchant of French descent who Anglicized his name to John before moving to Concord in 1799.

Snowshoe hare (*Lepus americanus*). One of these burrowed under Thoreau's house to live. (© Geostock/ Photodisc/Getty Images)

Since its 1941 inception, the Thoreau Society has grown into the largest literary society devoted to any American author. It's much larger than the Emerson Society, which piggybacks on the Thoreau Society's annual gathering. Today, the meeting is attended by hundreds and extends through several days of sessions, field trips, banquets, and theatrical and musical events. Its members are a fascinating mix of writers, academics, hobbyists, educators, business people, young professionals, and retirees. The interested public is also welcome.

The House Site lies just inside the east rim of a south-facing hollow. This location satisfied Thoreau's declaration of April 5, 1841: "I will build my lodge on the southern slope of some hill." Four years later he did just that, choosing a south-facing clearing, a sunny patch surrounded by vigorously growing young trees that had sprouted twenty years earlier. During early winter and early spring this warm patch was often a dun-colored island of thawed ground surrounded by a sea of white snow. Henry remarked that his house stayed warm, even when his fire went out.

In late March 1845, Thoreau borrowed an axe, walked down the tracks, took a trail to this hollow, and felled a few of the young pines. Within a month, he had hewed them into timbers six inches square and joined them together to create the walls and floor of what would be his one-room house. Within two months, rumors about Thoreau's experiment in deliberate living had become a staple of community gossip. In May he invited his friends to a house-raising party to lift the framed sides up onto the floor and tie them together with a ridge beam. Among those who helped celebrate were Ralph Waldo Emerson; William Ellery Channing; Bronson Alcott; Edmund Hosmer and sons John, Edmund, and Andrew; and the two Curtis boys, George and Burrill. When Henry finally moved in on July 4, 1845, his house was little more than a timber frame sheathed with boards recycled from the shanty of an Irish railroad worker, James Collins. The remaining construction would gradually take place over the next few months as the shingles, windows, and the door appeared. The fireplace and chimney were built just before freeze-up.

Today, the house footprint is marked by a series of nine granite posts. Heavy chain is draped between them to outline a rectangle fifteen feet long and ten feet wide. The single gap in the chain marks the presumed location of the door, centered between the corners on the southeast side. That gap invites visitors to imagine walking inside a small wooden house that's no longer there. Sophia's sketch of the house suggests that the door may have been offset to the west.

Now that we're geographically located, let's imagine plopping the house replica from our first stop down onto the house footprint of this stop. Henry's door opened to the southeast, his fireplace vented northwesterly, and his pair of large windows opened northeast and southwest. Based on *Walden,* his desk was placed to the left below the western window. To the right was his cot, where he slept between dark and dawn. In the middle lay the wooden floor where Henry's overnight visitors may have slept on a bedroll. Two particular guests, a poet and a philosopher, were featured in a script inserted into *Walden'*s chapter "Former Inhabitants; and Winter Visitors." The poet was William Ellery Channing, who stayed

## The quiet whoosh of a falling sumac

"The sumach (*Rhus glabra*) grew luxuriantly about the house, pushing up through the embankment which I had made, and growing five or six feet the first season . . . and sometimes, as I sat at my window, so heedlessly did they grow and tax their weak joints, I heard a fresh and tender bough suddenly fall like a fan to the ground, when there was not a breath of air stirring, broken off by its own weight."

The disturbed soils of the House Site were perfect habitat for sumac. The phrase "fall like a fan" suggests a quiet whooshing sound that could nevertheless be heard above the stillness of that day.

about two weeks and claims to have slept under Thoreau's bed frame. The philosopher was Bronson Alcott, who spent multiple winter nights. Many unnamed others stayed as well, including at least one runaway slave. On one famous night, the house was unoccupied because Thoreau had been jailed for an act of civil disobedience: refusing to pay his poll tax.

☙ ❧

Thoreau cut and hewed white pine timbers to frame his house. The angled end of this worm-eaten timber suggests it supported the roof gables. Note the nails. (Courtesy of the Walden Woods Project)

Thoreau could have built his house anywhere in this sunny hollow. So why did he locate his house where he did? Why did he align it southeasterly? Why did he build it so far from the lake? No specific answers to these questions are known from his writings, correspondence, or first-person accounts from those who knew him.

Perhaps transportation was the key. Henry's choice split the difference among three points of interest: southerly to the lake, northwesterly to the railroad in the direction of his family, and northeasterly to Walden Street in the direction of town center.

Another possibility was the soil.

> I dug my cellar in the side of a hill sloping to the south, where a woodchuck had formerly dug his burrow, down through sumach and blackberry roots, and the lowest stain

> of vegetation, six feet square by seven deep, to a fine sand
> where potatoes would not freeze in any winter . . . It was but
> two hours' work . . . The house is still but a sort of porch at the
> entrance of a burrow.

Taking Thoreau at his word, he sited his house where he knew the digging would be easy. The clean, white, cobble-free sand at the mouth of a woodchuck's burrow signaled easy work relative to the stony soils common nearby. Additionally, the roots of blackberries and sumacs near the burrow would have been easier to cut through than the roots of oak and pine.

The alignment of the house is an even greater mystery. Based on Thoreau's exacting survey map and on a line drawn perpendicular to the fireplace foundation by Roland Robbins, the length of the house was oriented south-southeast at roughly 150 degrees. Henry's only door opened toward the eastern edge of Thoreau's Cove, but with a view in that direction limited by a low hillock. Nothing about the terrain precluded Henry from creating a good water view toward the south, yet he chose not to do so. Was this intentional?

Perhaps he wanted his door to point toward the morning sun. Perhaps he wanted to maximize solar absorption by facing his house corner to the south. Perhaps he wanted to maximize his southwesterly window view over what he variously called his "clearing" or "yard." Perhaps he wanted to align the length of the house parallel to the contour of the slope, which is architecturally most efficient. Perhaps ventilation was the key: his chosen orientation allowed breezes concentrated by Thoreau's Cove to enter the house's door, its largest opening, before being drawn out both side windows.

Once installed, Thoreau's large western window framed a good view over a small clearing in the hollow. In its midst was his chaotic wood pile, which reminded him of the "pleasing work" of converting pitch pine stumps into fuel. Morning after morning he sat at his desk below that window, laboring on his many manuscripts. Like all writers, he would occasionally glance up, in this case to a scene of wood chips, flowers, perennial shrubs, and animal activity. One of these glances is captured in *Walden:* "As I sit at my window this summer afternoon, hawks are circling about my clearing." His writing life was indeed a *Life in the Woods,* and not a life on the water.

> Sometimes, in a summer morning, having taken my accustomed bath, I sat in my sunny doorway from sunrise till noon, rapt in a revery, amidst the pines and hickories and sumachs, in undisturbed solitude and stillness, while the birds sing around or flitted noiseless through the house, until by the sun falling in at my west window, or the noise of some traveller's wagon on the distant highway, I was reminded of the lapse of time.

## Smooth sumac
### (*Rhus glabra*)

"Its broad pinnate tropical leaf was pleasant though strange to look on . . . In August, the large masses of berries, which, when in flower, had attracted many wild bees, gradually assumed their bright velvety crimson hue, and by their weight again bent down and broke the tender limbs."

Smooth sumac has dense clusters of beautiful berries that attract birds, which readily and widely disperse the seeds. Sumac is a weedy shrub that thrives on disturbed sandy soils like the low embankment Thoreau created to level his House Site. Thoreau specifically identified the species as the smooth sumac, a species still found on the park's plant inventory.

Though he describes scenes through both his door and west window from inside the house, he doesn't mention a water view. Indeed, from a sitting position at his desk, no water was visible through the door and only a small slice of distant Ice Fort Cove could be seen. Yet, immediately beyond his doorway, Thoreau's cone of vision over the water expanded greatly and was nicely centered over Walden's most circular and largest kettle, the western basin. From that doorway viewpoint, the central and eastern basins are blocked by the ridge of Bare Peak. Importantly, the distant horizon of the "shrub-oak plateau to which the opposite shore arose," was an upward view.

Henry had lots of animal company at his house: "squirrels on the roof and under the floor, a whip-poor-will on the ridge-pole, a blue jay screaming beneath the window, a hare or woodchuck under the house, a screech owl or a cat owl behind it, a flock of wild geese or a laughing loon on the pond, and a fox to bark in the night." These animal companions, and the plants of the nearby woods, contrasted sharply with the more common flora and fauna of the open fields and pastures that dominated his rural Middlesex countryside:

> Not even a lark or an oriole, those mild plantation birds, ever visited my clearing. No cockerels to crow nor hens to cackle in the yard. No yard! But unfenced nature reaching up to your very sills. A young forest growing up under your meadows, and wild sumachs and blackberry vines breaking through into your cellar; sturdy pitch pines rubbing and creaking against the shingles for want of room, their roots reaching quite under the house . . . no gate—no front-yard— and no path to the civilized world.

When Thoreau lived at Walden, virtually all of his nonsleeping indoor time was spent reading, writing, and editing. Counterintuitively, the bulk of his writing time went to projects other than *Walden.* Most urgent was the memorial to his brother, later titled *A Week on the Concord and Merrimack Rivers.* He wrote at least one full draft of this "big book" about rivers while sitting in the woods. There, he also wrote the lion's share of *The Maine Woods,* half a dozen other essays and hundreds of lengthy private journal passages. Based on final word count, approximately half of *Walden* was written at Walden.

❦ ❧

The foundation of Thoreau's one-room house was a study in archaeology even before he died. This fossilization process began on September 6, 1847, when Henry walked away to live in the much grander Emerson house in town, having been invited by the lady of the house, Lidian Emerson. There, Thoreau spent a month living with her husband Ralph, the children, and many visitors before the master left for a lengthy European lecture tour. This arrangement made Henry the "man of the house" for twelve continuous months, a plan that worked perhaps too well: he became emotionally attached to both the house and wife.

Thoreau's departure from the pond left a two-year-new, structurally sound house on Emerson's woodlot. With charity in mind, Emerson "bought" this house from Henry and leased it on September 28, 1847, to Hugh Whelan, his Scottish gardener. The following January, Whelan used some sort of livestock power to move the house off its foundation and up into Henry's former Bean Field near Walden Street. Next to the relocated house, Whelan dug a cellar and gathered stones for a new foundation to put it on. Some of those stones were undoubtedly recycled from Thoreau's foundation.

All that remained of Henry's former house was a cellar hole, a landform Thoreau affectionately called a "dent in the earth." At some point this dent was intentionally filled with loads of earth, perhaps to keep animals and people from falling into it. Four years after Henry's departure, on November 30, 1851, he described his former home as being "indistinct as an old cellar hole," with nothing remaining but a "faint indentation" with caved-in edges. "Where is my home?" he asked plaintively. Inspired by this and other nearby house ruins, Thoreau retroactively peopled the woods of *Walden* in a new chapter: "Former Inhabitants; and Winter Visitors."

> For human society I was obliged to conjure up the former occupants of these woods. Within the memory of many of my townsmen the road near which my house stands resounded with the laugh and gossip of inhabitants, and the woods which border it were notched and dotted here and there with their little gardens and dwellings, though it was then much more shut in by the forest than now.

One of the abandoned dwellings was a one-room cabin belonging to a woman named Zilpah White, a freed slave who lived along Walden Street near the turn of the nineteenth century. Another domicile was the cellar of "Cato Ingraham, slave of Duncan Ingraham, Esquire, gentleman, of Concord village, who built his slave a house, and gave him permission to live in Walden Woods." The farthest ruin was that of Brister Freeman, a slave of squire Cummings, and Freeman's wife, Fenda the fortune teller. The nearest ruin was where "Wyman the potter squatted, and furnished his townsmen with earthenware, and left descendants to succeed him."

Owing to family troubles, Whelan left town, leaving Thoreau's relocated empty house very near Walden Street. Consequently, in September 1849, Emerson sold the building to the Clark brothers, who hauled it across town for use as a granary. In 1868, after spending nearly twenty years as a corncrib, the house that Henry built was dismantled for its boards and shingles. Fragments of the house have since become valuable souvenirs that are eagerly sought by Thoreau aficionados. Collections of these materials—bricks, nails, shingles, timbers, and glass—are now on exhibit in local museums and historic sites, notably the Concord Museum and the Walden Woods Project's Thoreau Institute.

Today Thoreau's memorial cairn is a sprawling mound of stones over twenty feet long and ten feet wide. For the three decades of my experience, its size and shape have been changing like a great stone amoeba. And for the last decade, its smaller surface stones are being rearranged into vertical, whisker-like stacks that rob the site of the simplicity Thoreau valued so highly. Though the cairn appears as if it has been there forever, its present incarnation was dumped from the back of a truck in 1978.

The process of memorializing Thoreau's House Site began with Bronson Alcott and his daughter Abigail May in September 1863, sixteen months after Thoreau's death on May 6, 1862. Fifteen years after the building's removal in 1848, they noted that "the grounds are much overgrown with shrubbery, and the site of the hermitage is almost obliterated." Later, Thoreau's frequent sojourning companion, William Ellery Channing, noted that the exact location was becoming blurred somewhere along "the pathway to the pond." This would change in June 1872 when Mrs. Mary Newbury Adams of Dubuque, Iowa, inaugurated the memorial cairn to commemorate the site. She had been in town visiting the Emersons when Bronson Alcott stopped by on his way to the Unitarian Church picnic at Walden Pond. Mrs. Adams joined him for the walk and relayed the experience to her daughter, who later described it this way:

> When they reached the spot where Thoreau's little house used to stand, mother said it was a pity there was nothing to mark the place, so strangers might know it. "Well," said Mr. Alcott, "a cut stone would hardly be appropriate, would it, for Thoreau?" She suggested building a cairn and then let everyone who loved Thoreau add a stone and said she was going to start it right then. She got a stone and with a little improvised ceremony laid it down in her own name. Then Mr. Alcott got one for himself and one for Mrs. Alcott.

Emerson laid his cobble-stone the following day. Alcott had known exactly where the house had been because he had helped raise its frame twenty-seven years earlier, in 1845. He was Thoreau's very good friend,

Thoreau's cairn at Stop 8, House Site, in the early twentieth century. The view toward the left is roughly in alignment with the former house. (Courtesy of the Thoreau Society, The Thoreau Society Archives at the Walden Woods Project's Thoreau Institute Library)

described in *Walden* as "one of the last of the philosophers . . . I think that he must be the man of the most faith of any alive."

Mrs. Adams and Mr. Alcott began their cairn near the former front door of the house. Over the years, it became a growing cone of loose stone. A bronze plaque was later affixed to a nearby boulder to communicate what was being marked. By the late 1870s, pilgrims were coming from afar, often escorted by Ralph Waldo Emerson, Bronson Alcott, Ellery Channing, Frank Sanborn, or Fred Hosmer. Writer John Burroughs came in 1877. Poet Walt Whitman made his pilgrimage in 1881. Pioneering conservationist John Muir arrived in 1883 with his dog-eared copy of *Walden* in hand. Muir, who helped create our national park system, was a lifelong devotee of Thoreau.

The memorial cairn of stones at the House Site today is younger than July 7, 1978. Three years earlier, and without consulting the Thoreau Society, the park director had the previous cairn trucked away because he thought it looked ugly. When the Thoreau Society learned that their sacred memorial had gone missing, their howls of protest forced the director to rethink his decision. With reluctance, the state of Massachusetts trucked the stones back to create the modern mound.

One of the oddest things about Thoreau's House Site is that its location was rumored to have been lost, even though Thoreau had accurately surveyed and published its location in *Walden,* and even though a cairn had long marked the exact spot. In 1922, a young visitor named Wade Van Dore dug a hole to verify the house's former existence. "Using my hatchet for a shovel," he wrote, "I dug behind the cairn until I found the base of broken bricks and stones Thoreau had described using for his fireplace chimney. Extracting a half-brick to keep, I carefully refilled the hole."

Nine years later, in 1931, the future first president of the Thoreau Society, Raymond Adams, accompanied by local resident Raymond Emerson, marked the corners of the sagging cellar hole depression with four posts of cut granite. The choice of cut, quarried granite to mark the House Site is shocking because Thoreau detested the use of this material for monuments, which he saw as a manifestation of vanity and income inequality. Before steam drilling, cut stone was called *hammered stone* because it was cut with a hammer and chisel, usually by unpaid or low-paid laborers to create monuments to the wealthy and powerful. Thoreau was very clear about his preferences in *Walden:*

> Nations are possessed with an insane ambition to perpet-
> uate the memory of themselves by the amount of hammered
> stone they leave . . . More sensible is a rod of stone wall that
> bounds an honest man's field than a hundred-gated Thebes
> that has wandered farther from the true end of life . . . Most
> of the stone a nation hammers goes toward its tomb only. It
> buries itself alive.

Fifty-eight years earlier, Bronson Alcott had understood and sym-
pathized with Henry's dislike for cut stone. This is why he encour-
aged Mrs. Adams to memorialize Thoreau's legacy with the natural
cobbles used to build stone walls—not hammered stone. Later, he
described the "rude stones" of the cairn as "a monument more fitting
than the costliest carving."

New England's great 1938 hurricane took a serious toll on Henry's House Site. The tall white pines Henry had planted near the
future site of the cairn were blown down. The following year, a
*Walden*-smitten young author named E. B. White made his pilgrimage to the House Site, writing Henry a posthumous personal letter:

> Your front yard is marked by a bronze tablet set in a stone.
> Four small granite posts, a few feet away, show where the
> house was . . . Back of it is a pile of stones, a sort of cairn, left
> by your visitors as a tribute I suppose. It is a rather ugly little
> heap of stones . . .

White noticed that someone had built a fire in the depression
over Thoreau's former cellar and tossed beer bottles into the charcoal and ash. White's visit seems to have coincided with a low point
in the history of the House Site.

The July 4, 1945, centennial celebration of Thoreau's move to
Walden Pond brought Lincoln resident Roland Robbins to the House

Replica of Thoreau's green writing desk with manuscript pages, writing implements, and a small lamp, all set up in their customary positions below the western window within the house replica. (Props courtesy of Richard Smith, January 2013)

Site for the first time. By November, and with the encouragement of the Thoreau Society, he had moved the sprawling cairn downhill and shovel-excavated the soil. There he found bricks and the lower part of the mortared house foundation intact, confirming Thoreau's construction narrative. The foundation was less a continuous wall of stones then masses mortared together, especially at the corners and below the chimney.

Robbins published his account of the excavation under the title

*Discovery at Walden.* His discovery applies mainly to the recovery of additional artifacts, especially nails, brick fragments, cairn stones, and the chimney foundation. It does not apply to the location and orientation of the house, which had been approximately marked by the corner posts of Raymond Adams, which bounded the depression described by E. B. White, which coincided with the excavation of Van Dore, which occurred at the exact spot where Bronson Alcott and friends marked the site with a stone cairn, which is where Bronson remembered raising the house.

After Robbins's House Site excavation, the decision was made by the Thoreau Society to mark the footprint with a proper monument. Shortly thereafter, Concord resident and renowned architect T. Mott Shaw designed a memorial consisting of nine large, cut-granite posts linked together with a draping chain. On March 28, 1948, the society installed it, moving Adams's smaller cut-stone posts north to mark the footprint of the woodshed, for a grand total of thirteen granite posts.

These cut-stone posts seem wrong. Donation of the land to create Walden Pond State Reservation required that the property be maintained as the "Walden of Thoreau and Emerson." This mandate was upheld by the Massachusetts State Supreme Judicial Court in 1960, when they "ordered the commissioners [of Middlesex County] to abide by the deed restrictions, using Thoreau's celebrated work *Walden* as a guide to the Reservation's proper management." The thirteen posts of hammered stone appear to violate the Supreme Court's mandate to use "*Walden* as a guide" when making management decisions.

Three important trails converged on Thoreau's House Site. The most well-beaten headed south to the lake. In *Walden* (1854), he describes this trail's persistence into the early 1850s, long after his 1847 departure.

> I had not lived there a week before my feet wore a path from my door to the pond-side; and though it is five or six years since I trod it, it is still quite distinct. It is true, I fear, that others may have fallen into it, and so helped to keep it open.

Henry's second well-beaten trail headed northwest toward the railroad tracks. This was his corridor for heading home to visit his family. His third trail was northward and uphill to the flats of the Bean Field, where his path joined a carriage path to Walden Street, now Route 126. This third trail offered Henry a path toward Concord Center and Emerson's house.

Thoreau's many visitors used all three trails when they visited between 1845 and 1847. For Henry, these trails were equivalent to the access streets and driveways leading to present-day suburban houses. They provided access to the people of his life: "I had more visitors while I lived in the woods than at any other period in my life," he wrote. Lucky for us, Thoreau's three trails are still well maintained by park staff. We can walk in his footsteps to his former front door and give him an imagined hello.

## Sophia Thoreau fought slavery in 1846.

Henry's younger sister, Sophia, was an important presence in his life and became a vigorous guardian of his posthumous literary legacy. Her link to the House Site is twofold. First, she visited her brother there many times, initially because she worried for his safety. Second, the 1846 annual meeting of the Concord Female Anti-Slavery Society met at his house. Henry's mother (Cynthia) and sister (Sophia) helped lead the meeting. In *Walden,* Thoreau reported that "One real runaway slave, among the rest, whom I helped to forward toward the north star" overnighted in the house on the way to Canada.

We're finished with our longest stop. Our second of two detours off the Pond Path is at hand. Following Thoreau's trail to the north, we walk uphill from the house footprint. Approximately 150 feet beyond the granite posts, we'll notice the terrain flattening out abruptly. We will have returned to the top of the ancient delta plain for the first time since we walked down to the beach from the Terrace Edge.

Thoreau's friends chose natural cobbles (top) to commemorate his House Site. They avoided cut or "hammered stone" (bottom), which Henry disliked. The visible drill holes were used to cut the granite into regular pieces.

## AT A GLANCE

**Object:** The Bean Field today is a flat wooded plain west of Walden Street. For Thoreau it was a patch of good soil where he was "determined to know beans." His farming there in plain sight of the road was as an act of social theater.

**Location:** GPS coordinates 42° 26' 33.77" N, 71° 20' 33.81" W, 200 ft. These coordinates and the map location are to the nearest part of the flat plain above his House Site. We do not know how far back from Walden Street Thoreau's Bean Field extended.

**Moment:** The first horseless carriage known to have traversed Walden Street sputtered in front of the Bean Field in 1902. Named the "Red Devil," the car was driven by Mr. Warren of Lincoln.

The modern trail marks the former carriage path leading from Thoreau's Bean Field (to the left) down to Walden Pond, barely visible in the distance. Note flat terrace.

**Fun Fact:** Though described as a "briar patch," the Bean Field soil is officially mapped by the United States Natural Resource Conservation Service as the Windsor soil, one of the finest agricultural soils in all of New England.

**Nature:** In the Bean Field, Henry declared war on woodchucks, the most frequently mentioned animal in *Walden*.

# 9: BEAN FIELD

## Sense of Place

*Thoreau hand-planted and hand-cultivated a crop of white bush beans to demonstrate to the community how farming should be done. The length of his rows totaled seven miles. The patch of excellent soil he chose lies at the same level as the Visitor Center.*

We're back to flat. If we pirouette 360 degrees, we'll see nothing but trees, trails, and sky. We're back on the top of the ancient delta plain, the dust-covered abandoned floodplain of the glacial meltwater river that once flowed through and filled in the Walden Valley.

Now imagine this flat being covered not by century-old woods, but by seven miles of earthen furrows on a patch of land twice the size of a football field. Welcome to Thoreau's Bean Field, which lay just east of where we stand, but in a nearly identical natural setting. There he "planted about two acres and a

### Henry's Bean Field

"Before I finished my house, . . . I planted about two acres and a half of light and sandy soil near it chiefly with beans, but also a small part with potatoes, corn, peas, and turnips. The whole lot contains eleven acres . . . One farmer said that it was 'good for nothing but to raise cheeping squirrels on.'"

The "light and sandy soil" of the Bean Field was actually an excellent soil officially mapped as the Windsor soil. At Walden, this loamy soil is composed of sandy dust blown by strong glacial winds from the abandoned channels of the ancient delta plain.

half of upland," a "yellow gravelly upland" bounded by a "shrub oak copse" at one end and a "blackberry field" on the other. Note his emphasis on the word "upland." To get to his Bean Field, Thoreau had to climb up out of the great hollow of Walden Pond.

With hoe in hand, Henry walked sideways between seemingly endless rows of tender beans. On his head was a broad hat to ward off the sun. When working this field, Henry was being a stage actor playing the role of a "good" farmer in the social theater of town life. The script of his one-act play became a chapter of *Walden* that may seem strangely out of place to a first reader, but makes perfect sense for those who know the book well.

More so than any other chapter, "The Bean-Field" links Thoreau's deliberate remove from society with his deliberate exposure to it. When cultivating the field, he straddled the borderland between his solitary life in the woods and his blatant exposure to the main highway between Concord and Lincoln. He was especially visible when he hired an ox team and a man to pull out the stumps and plow the furrows. He was regularly visible when he spent

## Woodchucks were Henry's woodland friends and agricultural enemies.

"I came to love my rows, my beans, though so many more than I wanted. They attached me to the earth . . . My auxiliaries are the dews and rains which water this dry soil, and what fertility is in the soil itself, which for the most part is lean and effete. My enemies are worms, cool days, and most of all woodchucks."

Also known as the groundhog, this large rodent forages in broad daylight at ground level, keeping within easy reach of its burrow, making it easily seen. Thoreau mentions this species (*Marmota monax*) twenty times in *Walden*. In his Bean Field, woodchucks nibbled his crop as fast as it grew. On one occasion, Thoreau killed and roasted one as a dietary experiment. Henry sited his house directly over a woodchuck's burrow because the sand looked easy to dig into. Though these fat rodents hibernate in winter, Thoreau says nothing about their rumored ability to predict how long winter will last.

Woodchucks (*Marmota monax*). These were common daylight companions for Thoreau. (© Little Things/iStockphoto/Getty Images)

up to seven hours per day doing manual labor in an open agricultural field in plain sight of every roadside traveler. His townsmen hailed him as they passed, and he hailed them in return.

Thoreau described the daily grind of becoming well-acquainted with beans: "When they were growing, I used to hoe from five o'clock in the morning till noon," working "barefooted, dabbling like a plastic artist in the dewy and crumbling sand . . . pacing slowly backward and forward," and "making the earth say beans instead of grass—this was my daily work."

His philosophical goal was to show that the old-fashioned, intimate practice of agricultural husbandry was far, far better than the stressful nineteenth-century practice of producing larger quantities of market commodities for sale in a capitalistic system. The latter practice, he thought, was as damaging to the land as it was to the human soul: "the landscape is deformed, husbandry is degraded with us, and the farmer leads the meanest of lives. He knows Nature but as a robber." Thoreau also wanted to illustrate self-reliance by growing food he would eat, namely, the potatoes, turnips, peas, and two kinds of corn he planted as well.

The earth he worked with his hoe spoke also of the civilizations that predated his in the preceding millennia.

## The sharp tinkle of steel hoe against small stones and tools

"As I drew a still fresher soil about the rows with my hoe, I disturbed the ashes of unchronicled nations who in primeval years lived under these heavens, and their small implements of war and hunting were brought to the light of this modern day . . . When my hoe tinkled against the stones, that music echoed to the woods and the sky, and was an accompaniment to my labor which yielded an instant and immeasurable crop."

Archaeologists still excavate with metal trowels similar to the blade of Thoreau's hoe. Both tools make a lovely metallic sound when striking stone artifacts. In loamy soils like those of the Bean Field, each clink is the sound of discovery.

As I drew a still fresher soil about the rows with my hoe, I disturbed the ashes of unchronicled nations who in primeval years lived under these heavens, and their small implements of war and hunting were brought to the light of this modern day. They lay mingled with other natural stones, some of which bore the marks of having been burned by Indian fires, and some by the sun, and also bits of pottery and glass brought hither by the recent cultivators of the soil.

His stones were storied with deep time: rounded cobblestones from ice-age streams, campfire stones from unknown peoples, sharp-edged stone tools from arrowheads to adzes, stoneware pottery of native and European style, and glass from the last century or two.

The Bean Field had only recently been harvested of its trees by Tommy Wyman, the previous landowner. To get his logs out, Wyman had improved the "carriage road" to very near the House Site. Wyman's stumps and an abandoned rail fence became Thoreau's most important sources of fuel, which he happily sacrificed to Vulcan, the Roman god of fire.

Thoreau's choice of where to plant shows his nose for soil quality. The good patch of soil he chose was surrounded by far worse soils. This soil was later mapped by soil scientists as the Windsor soil, a type named after the town of Windsor, Connecticut, located within the colonial agricultural Eden of the lower Connecticut River Valley. The Windsor soil is so good for crops that it was claimed by Connecticut as its official state soil. In both settings—Walden and Windsor—loamy dust blown from broad delta plains settled on the ground when the ice-age winds died down. For Thoreau, this soil was like moist frosting on a dry cake of gravel.

Thoreau's crop was the "small common white bush bean." He hand-planted them in rows about fifteen rods long and three feet apart. This pattern, applied to two and a half acres—or 108,900 square feet—requires approximately 147 rows, each about 248 feet long. The total length would have been 36,300 feet or 6.88 miles. In *Walden*, Thoreau reported a similar length of "seven miles." Quite clearly, he was "determined to know beans."

Henry started his oversized garden project more than a month before he began occupying his house on July 4, 1845. Consequently, he must have been commuting daily from town by foot for the first month via the railroad tracks. Mornings were devoted to beans; afternoons to house construction; evenings to friends and family.

"But why should I raise them?" Thoreau asked himself of his beans. "Only Heaven knows," was his rhetorical answer. "This was my curious labor all summer." Here, Thoreau is being his usual

## Hickory
### (*Carya* sp.)

"Instead of singing like the birds, I silently smiled at my incessant good fortune. As the sparrow had its trill, sitting on the hickory before my door, so had I my chuckle or suppressed warble which he might hear out of my nest."

Though less common than pine or oak, hickories are so common on the region's sandy soils that the triad *oak-pine-hickory* is used to describe the natural forest type. Thoreau specifically mentioned that hickories grew in the woods at the edge of the Bean Field, possibly *C. glabra*, the pignut hickory.

**Hugh Whelan moved Thoreau's house in 1848.**

In January 1848, a Scottish immigrant named Hugh Whelan yanked Thoreau's house off its foundation and dragged it up into the Bean Field, where it sat empty for eighteen months. Whelan had leased the house the previous September from Ralph Waldo Emerson, for whom he worked as a gardener. Whelan dug a new cellar hole and gathered stones for a new house foundation but never finished the job, leaving town instead. Emerson then sold the empty one-room building to the Clark brothers, who dragged it across town to use as a corncrib.

cryptic self. Historian Robert Gross answered Thoreau's question in his essay "The Great Bean Field Hoax: Thoreau and the Agricultural Reformers." In summary, Gross wrote: "The account of that venture . . . purports to represent a true experience . . . But as with everything in *Walden,* it is more than that . . . [it's] . . . an elaborate spoof."

Nobody else in Concord grew beans for a living. Thoreau's eccentric choice of crop had many motivations: a celebration of Native American horticulture, a visible protest against capitalistic commodity farming, and a humorous poke at society for its "Yankee conservativism."

*Walden*'s long opening chapter is titled "Economy." In it, we learn how efficient Thoreau was at home economics. In the "Bean-Field" chapter, we learn that his agricultural economics were pathetic. Despite using an exorbitant amount of seed, Thoreau's yield was only seven or eight bushels per acre, one third that of a normal crop, in part because he refused to apply fertilizer, then called manure. And after two months of hard field labor comparable to self-inflicted chain-gang work, his "pecuniary profit" was only $8.71. By contrast, Henry's literary economics in the Bean Field were an overflowing cornucopia because he labored not for profit but "for the sake of tropes and expression, to serve a parable-maker one day." The result was a "perfectly cultivated acre."

As social theater, Thoreau's Bean Field was an agricultural commune of one. It shouted out the same messages about honest labor, self-sufficiency, and self-culture, a defining tenet of transcendentalism being broadcast by other social utopian experiments such as George Ripley's Brook Farm and Bronson Alcott's Fruitlands.

Henry decided to let his large 1845 field go fallow for the next two summers of his Walden sojourn, planting only a third of an acre in 1846, and none in 1847. Given the initial capital expense, shutting down his performance early was akin to closing a Broadway show before the end of its run.

Within a few years, Thoreau's Bean Field had deteriorated to a brushy sod. In April 1859, Henry, hired as a day laborer, planted trees in that sod instead of beans in furrows—400 white pines and 100 larches set out in straight rows. Moving ahead to 1896, many of those trees burned down. In 1938, the great hurricane toppled the rest. Today, we're back to weedy pines and oaks on a dry plateau.

Throughout, the carriage road next to the Bean Field remained the main access to Thoreau's Cove for wandering romantics and pilgrims. H. W. Gleason photographed the dusty road in 1914. Edward Emerson mapped it in 1920. Despite this clear documentation and mapping, Thoreau scholars of the mid-twentieth century disagreed about where Thoreau's Bean Field had been.

Leaving the Bean Field, we now retrace our steps down toward the lake. On the way we'll pass between the house footprint and the cairn. When we reach the Pond Path at the lake perimeter, we will turn right and start looking for one of several smaller paths down to the gravelly shore. Taking one of those paths, we'll cross the gravelly beach to the water line. Thoreau's Cove lies to our left. The main part of the lake—the western basin—lies straight ahead. We've arrived at our next stop.

## AT A GLANCE

**Object:** The Waterfront is what Thoreau called his "pond-side." Nowadays it's a rounded shelf of gravel projecting into the west side of Thoreau's Cove.

**Location:** GPS coordinates 42° 26' 21.75" N, 71° 20' 32.58" W, 154 ft. A short, downhill walk from the House Site brings us to the Pond Path. After turning right (west) for less than 100 feet, we take the first pathway down to the left onto an open gravel surface.

**Moment:** In late autumn 1868, an eccentric named Stuart Hotham dug into the slope above the Waterfront and built a small wooden structure to live through the winter. He was dubbed "Thoreau's Successor."

**Fun Fact:** Behind Thoreau's "pond-side" is an unusually small, circular structure

May Alcott's sketch of Thoreau rowing a boat at his "pond-side," our Waterfront stop. (May Alcott, "Walden, Thoreau's 'pond-side,'" from *Concord Sketches*, 1869; courtesy of the Concord Free Public Library)

visible on laser imagery (LiDAR) that appears to be a rimmed pool that was later abandoned, vegetated, and partially filled by sediment. In his *Journal*, Thoreau mentioned it at least six times, but doesn't interpret its purpose.

**Nature:** This was Thoreau's favorite place for watching migrating waterfowl. Loons, geese, and various types of ducks preferred the large western basin, where they were safest from hunters' guns.

# 10: WATERFRONT

## Sense of Place

*From this Waterfront, Thoreau enjoyed water views, watched wildlife, dipped his drinking water, and went boating, swimming, and fishing on land owned by Cyrus Hubbard. From this shore, the western basin of Walden Pond appears roughly circular.*

n the opening line of *Walden; or, Life in the Woods,* Thoreau claims to have lived "on the shore of Walden Pond." This claim exaggerates the proximity between his house "in the woods" and his Waterfront "on the shore," where he officiated his own religious services: "I got up early and bathed in the pond; that was a religious exercise, and one of the best things which I did."

Where, exactly, was Thoreau's shoreline access? The nearest water was at the tip of Thoreau's Cove only 190 feet away from his door. Unfortunately, the water at that point was very shallow and sometimes muddy, weedy, warm, and stagnant. Consequently, Thoreau walked at least twice that distance to a rounded, gravelly shore jutting into the western side of Thoreau's Cove. Henry called it his "pond-side." Photographer H. W. Gleason called it "Thoreau's Point." This guide uses the term "Waterfront," which is both more accurate and more specific. There, Thoreau found a firm gravel beach with access to Thoreau's Cove on the left and to a steep shore face that plunged straight ahead into the clean, deep water of the western basin. This site was a whopping 432 feet from his front door, not

Canada geese (*Branta canadensis*). During Thoreau's era, flocks of geese rested on Walden during their seasonal migrations. (© Russell Illig/Photodisc/Getty Images)

counting curves in the trail. This exceeds the distance of a football field, including both end zones.

Whereas Henry Thoreau lived in the woods from 1845 to 1847, an interesting character named Stuart Hotham lived on the shore directly behind the Waterfront in 1868. Hotham was a cash-poor divinity student from New York City who decided that a monkish year at Walden Pond would help prepare him for missionary work. So, with Ralph Waldo Emerson's permission, he built a shack dug into the slope of a shoreline promontory. The *New York Times* described Hotham as "Thoreau's Successor—The New Hermit at Walden Pond." Emerson described him as a "tall, reserved, and homely looking" retired sailor and "an eccentric naval officer." A quiet vegetarian, Hotham managed to survive one winter and spring before leaving quietly, apparently driven out by too much attention. His mistake was to build directly above the water where he could be seen by all and visited by many.

Thoreau's many "pond-side" descriptions in *Walden* locate him exactly at the Waterfront. "I have my horizon bounded by woods all to myself; a distant view of the railroad where it touches the pond on the one hand, and of the fence which skirts the woodland road on the other." The cone of vision he described coincides exactly with the cone of vision at our Waterfront stop. He also located this point exactly when he surveyed the lake in 1846: from it he drew twelve lines raying out in all directions.

Thoreau's pathway between house and pond also locates the Waterfront exactly. In *Walden*'s "Conclusion" he wrote: "I had not lived there a week before my feet wore a path from my door to the pond-side." This path description is independently confirmed by two nineteenth-century sketches. Abigail May Alcott sketched

## Canada geese circled in large honking flocks.

"As it grew darker, I was startled by the honking of geese flying low over the woods, like weary travellers getting in late from southern lakes, and . . . with hushed clamor wheeled and settled in the pond. So I came in, and shut the door, and passed my first spring night in the woods. In the morning I watched the geese from the door through the mist, sailing in the middle of the pond, fifty rods off, so large and tumultuous that Walden appeared like an artificial pond for their amusement. But when I stood on the shore they at once rose up with a great flapping of wings at the signal of their commander, and when they had got into rank circled about over my head, twenty-nine of them, and then steered straight to Canada, with a regular honk from the leader at intervals, trusting to break their fast in muddier pools."

Henry loved the great flocks of Canada geese (*Branta canadensis*) that circled down to Walden Pond to rest during their migrations. These gregarious creatures provided a counterpoint to the solitude-preferring loons. When Thoreau reached the Waterfront, the geese flew away. Canada geese are mainly grazers of grass and grain, but they also forage on aquatic plants. Since Thoreau's day, geese have become far less wary of humans. They remain in the region through the winter, thanks in part to climate warming.

## Henry's shoreline Waterfront

"I was seated by the shore of a small pond, about a mile and a half south of the village of Concord and somewhat higher than it, in the midst of an extensive wood between that town and Lincoln, . . . but I was so low in the woods that the opposite shore, half a mile off, like the rest, covered with wood, was my most distant horizon."

The view Thoreau described is probably not from his house on Ralph Waldo Emerson's land but from Thoreau's preferred Waterfront on Cyrus Hubbard's land. His passage emphasizes being "low in the woods" and "in the midst of an extensive wood," neither of which applies to his House Site.

from memory the lower part of Thoreau's path rising up from a rounded Waterfront and turning eastward. Thoreau's sister Sophia sketched the upper part of the same path on what became the frontispiece of *Walden*. Her sketch shows the path at Thoreau's front door turning westward away from the house before turning downward to the pond in a southerly direction. The two drawings link up to each other in the middle, confirming Thoreau's "pond-side" as our Waterfront.

Alcott's sketch does not show the unusual depression behind the beach at the Waterfront that Thoreau refers to in his *Journal* using a variety of names: "Hubbard's Pond-hole," "the pond-hole in Hubbard's woods," "the little meadow pool, or bay, in Hubbard's shore," "Cyrus Hubbard's basin," "the pondlet on Hubbard's land," and "that smaller pool by Walden in Hubbard's Wood." Pending an archaeological excavation, this former tiny "bay" was likely a small kettle with a southern rim that was strengthened and kept clear by ice-thrusting, and which may have been deepened for some prehistoric or early historic purpose. Today, a low stone wall rises above part of the rim.

At the Waterfront, Thoreau's horizontal field of view over the lake was at least twice as wide as that from his front yard. His vertical field of view was greater as well, rising from a sandy lake bottom up to the treetops on the opposite shore. From the Waterfront, Thoreau

could see all four of Walden's coves surrounding the central circle of its western basin: Thoreau's Cove to the left, Deep Cove straight across, Sandbank Cove across to the right, and Ice Fort Cove to the far right. From here, Thoreau's view resembled nearby White Pond, which Henry considered Walden's twin. Both have similar sizes, shapes, clarity, symmetry, and shorelines. For Thoreau, this part of Walden and all of White Pond were two "great crystals" of liquid light.

The Waterfront stop is the light-colored patch of gravel, here seen from across Thoreau's Cove. The pond surface is glazed with ice. Hubbard's "pondlet," the basin behind the gravel shore, has a raised rim.

A lake is the landscape's most beautiful and expressive feature. It is earth's eye; looking into which the beholder measures the depth of his own nature. The fluviatile trees next the

Willow (*Salix* spp.). Willows were a common sight for Thoreau around the pond shoreline. (© Florapix/Alamy)

shore are the slender eyelashes which fringe it, and the wooded hills and cliffs around are its overhanging brows.

It was almost certainly here that Henry looked down into the clear water, locked eyes with the lake, and asked: "Walden, is it you?" He didn't expect an answer. This was his way of animating, if not personifying, the lake. He and the lake were becoming good friends. It was here at the Waterfront that the attributes of the pond and the philosophical goals of its most famous resident converge most clearly.

Thoreau's enchantment with Walden's western basin, and the literary outcome of *Walden,* resulted from chance circumstance. Before meeting Ralph Waldo Emerson in 1837, Henry's youthful interest in nature had mainly involved boating, fishing, and hunting on his hometown's three rivers—the Assabet, Sudbury, and Concord. Though Walden Pond was on Henry's priority list of sojourning places, it wasn't central to his life. This changed during the years of Emerson's mentorship

(1837–1845) because Walden Pond was the favorite destination for the transcendentalist group. A modern path called the "Emerson-Thoreau Amble" approximates the route they often walked between Emerson's home and Thoreau's Cove.

When Thoreau ended his two-year sojourn in September 1847, he carried away a first draft of *Walden,* which, at that point, was a lecture in three parts titled "A History of Myself." At this stage the manuscript had been written by a transcendental utopian and societal critic. Indeed, Thoreau's three early drafts written between 1845 and 1847 had little to do with Walden Pond as a landform. At this stage, the pond was mainly a scenic backdrop for ideas and events that could have taken place almost anywhere: voluntary simplicity, truth, morality, fashion, health, independence, labor, slavery, technology, and political imperialism. Old-school Thoreau scholars were mainly interested in this early Thoreau, emphasizing his literary skills, political philosophy, and eccentric biography.

Astonishingly, old-school scholar Raymond Adams wrote: "Walden is not significant as a place at all. It is significant only because the word Walden suggests some thoughts a man had once. Where he had them doesn't really matter." This was the opinion of the Thoreau Society's first and longest-serving president, who guided scholarly thinking through 1955. He and his former graduate student Walter Harding

## Willow
### (*Salix* spp.)

"When the water is at its height, the alders, willows, and maples send forth a mass of fibrous red roots several feet long from all sides of their stems in the water, and to the height of three or four feet from the ground, in the effort to maintain themselves . . ."

The sediment texture of the stony shore at the Waterfront, combined with the fluctuating water table, made for perfect willow habitat. This family of tenacious, deciduous shrubs and small trees has over 400 species. Neither Thoreau's 1854 book nor the park's 2013 botanical inventory distinguish which willows are present.

> ## An old fisherman is humming a few psalms.
>
> "There was one older man, an excellent fisher and skilled in all kinds of woodcraft, who was pleased to look upon my house as a building erected for the convenience of fishermen . . . Once in a while we sat together on the pond, he at one end of the boat, and I at the other; but not many words passed between us, for he had grown deaf in his later years, but he occasionally hummed a psalm, which harmonized well enough with my philosophy."
>
> Thoreau moored and launched his boat from the Waterfront, possibly from the pondlet entrance at its southern margin. This passage describes a moonlit night of fishing over deep water. At such times, Thoreau felt like he had two heavens, one above the water and the other below.

promulgated an influential school of thought focused on the *person* who lived at the pond, and not the *pond* that inspired the person. Probably because the majority of the Thoreau Society's early presidents took their highest academic degrees in English, they prioritized the printed word over tangible physicality.

A "new school" accepts the emphasis of the old school as a starting place, but also wants to understand Thoreau as a curiosity-driven, self-taught natural scientist who leveraged his observations about the pond into great literature. By late 1851, Thoreau had become a gifted naturalist and lyrical nature writer inspired by reading widely in scientific travel literature, most notably Charles Darwin's *Voyage of the Beagle.* This new approach, in which philosophical truths emerge from scientific observations, caused Thoreau to reimagine his earlier manuscript, return frequently to Walden Pond on day trips, write four more drafts of *Walden,* and roughly double the book's size before publication in August 1854.

The *Walden* that resulted from this somewhat accidental infusion of natural science into his earlier experience at Walden Pond could only have been written about a kettle pond. Thoreau's original destination was probably Flint's Pond, where he had spent six idyllic weeks in 1837 with his college roommate, Charles Stearns.

In December 1841 Henry declared: "I want to go soon and live away by the pond where I shall hear only the wind whispering among the reeds." For Thoreau, Flint's Pond was "our greatest lake and inland sea," and was "comparatively shallow, and not remarkably pure." There one could "feel the wind blow on your cheek freely, and see the waves run" over a shallow rippled bottom, and enjoy the extensive reeds, or "rushes which grew in Indian file, in waving lines." But when Thoreau sought a place to build his house three years later, he instead opted for Walden Pond, where Emerson had recently purchased the Wyman Lot and given him permission to live there.

The result became literary history: a *Walden* about simplicity, humility, purity, resilience, and holism, rather than a *Flint's* about a marshy inland sea with inlet and outlet streams, darker waters, and farms leading to the water's edge.

From the Waterfront, Thoreau often imagined himself being at the lake's center, "withdrawn so far within the great ocean of solitude . . . [that] . . . only the finest sediment was deposited around me." The deepest and most tranquil part of Walden Pond lies directly below

> ### Abigail May Alcott Nieriker published a sketch in 1869.
>
> May Alcott, the daughter of Bronson and Abigail Alcott, and the sister of Louisa May Alcott, the well-known American author, was a young friend of Thoreau's. When a child, May (who was then called Abby) was often brought to visit Thoreau at his House Site by her father and sister. May's sketch of Thoreau in his rowboat below the Waterfront is the only eyewitness drawing of Thoreau at Walden Pond. She would have been only a few weeks shy of seven years old when Thoreau left the pond, so this sketch almost certainly was drawn from memory.

the center of the large western basin. There, at a depth of 102 feet, the water is as motionless as it is pitch black, giving rise to a sulfurous *dead zone* at the base. Microscopic bits of sediment, mainly

The foam results from dissolved chemicals introduced into the water by both natural processes and human impact.

aquatic plankton and pollen, rain down from above, remain undecayed for lack of oxygen, and thicken to create a soft, dark greenish-brown sediment called *muck*. Since the end of the last ice age, this process has created a lens-shaped deposit more than twelve feet thick. In 1979, lake scientist Marjorie Winkler investigated a sediment core taken from this muck. Using its archive of fossils, she reconstructed the history and prehistory of the larger lake. Since then, her work has been confirmed and refined by several recent studies.

One discovery showed a decline in the proportion of tree pollen and a rise in grass pollen. This documented the gradual clearing of the original old-growth forest, beginning with Puritan settlement in 1635. What had been about 90 percent forest was reduced to about 10 percent in Thoreau's era. Additionally, the sediment record for Thoreau's era revealed strong pulses of mineral silt and charcoal from logging and railroad operations.

Surprisingly, the clarity and low biological fertility of Walden's water remained virtually unchanged through the farming, railroad, and wood-cutting eras of history, and well into the twentieth century. Its transparency had resulted from many factors, especially the dearth of aquatic plankton due to the lack of dissolved organic nutrients, particularly phosphorous and nitrogen. Beginning in the early twentieth century, however, public swimming increased significantly, the nutrient content rose dramatically, and the clarity diminished.

By 1939 the lake had already become moderately enriched in nutrients, based on work by Edward Deevey, a pioneering lake scientist who noted Thoreau's contribution to limnology, a discipline not yet invented. On the day Deevey visited, he reported an estimated 1,000 swimmers on the beach. The number of swimmers and the degree of enrichment continued to increase into the 1970s when the decision was made to restrict attendance.

An astonishingly data-rich 2001 report by the U.S. Geological Survey has greatly refined our understanding. It ruled out a nearby landfill as a source of groundwater contamination and firmly established that the main source of extra nutrients contaminating the water in summer was human in origin. Swimmers were urinating into the lake, and groundwater from the wastewater treatment plant at park headquarters was seeping below the beach. These specific causes are being addressed and the situation is improving. One lingering concern involves the rise in the abundance of golden brown algae as a consequence of climate warming.

Leaving the water's edge, we now turn around and walk back over the gravel to the Pond Path. Turning left to the west, we will leave the second sector of our tour (northwest) to explore our third sector (southwest). The ambience quickly changes.

## SOUTHWEST: WALDEN'S STAR

As we leave Thoreau's Cove, the bank becomes very steep—so steep, in fact, that it has been difficult to maintain the Pond Path. During the six decades between when the trail was cut (1931–1935) and when it was restored (1986–1998), bank erosion had been very severe. Restoration required construction of a massive retaining wall of imported glacial boulders built around the headland between Thoreau's Cove, now behind us, and Ice Fort Cove, up ahead. The big stones are impossible to miss.

We're entering the southwest sector where the theme is "Walden's

The Pond Path heading toward Walden's western shore is bordered by a prominent retaining wall built of locally imported boulders.

Star." Here we will find a much more public world where the land was literally reshaped by the coming of the railroad and intensively used over a period of sixty years (1842–1902). This was before automobiles and highways shifted the activity to the northeast sector, which we've already toured.

Walking between Thoreau's Cove and Ice Fort Cove requires walking around a steep headland. This pattern of leapfrogging from cove to cove with a headland in between is one we'll repeat three times before we leave the southwest sector.

But for now, our goal is to reach the tip of the next cove.

## AT A GLANCE

**Object:** Ice Fort Cove lies immediately below the tracks of the Fitchburg Railroad. During the winter of 1846–1847, Thoreau watched ice harvesters build an enormous stack of ice there that resembled an old fort made of "azure-tinted marble."

**Location:** GPS coordinates 42° 26' 20.36" N, 71° 20' 41.86" W, 154 ft. The stop is the tip of the cove, defined as the place where the curvature of the shore is the same to left and right. Another way of locating the tip is to put the same amount of water on either side.

**Moment:** In 1843, one year after moving to Concord, Nathaniel Hawthorne described Ice Fort Cove as the "most beautiful cove of the whole lake."

**Fun Fact:** In the decades following the American Civil War (1861–1865), an

Boating at Lake Walden amusement park circa 1868. The view looks west over Ice Fort Cove. Note boulder-armored shoreline, swings, buildings, and gate below railroad tracks. (Courtesy of the Thoreau Society, The Thoreau Society Archives at the Walden Woods Project's Thoreau Institute Library)

occult movement known as Spiritualism became extremely popular in New England. During August 1869, one "camp meeting" at Ice Fort Cove had 160 tents.

**Nature:** Ice Fort Cove is normally the quietest cove on the lake, being the most well protected from the prevailing northwesterly winds. Aquatic insects—whirlygig beetles and water bugs—prefer its calm conditions.

# 11: ICE FORT COVE

## Sense of Place

*In 1847, Thoreau watched this part of Walden Pond become the site of industrial-scale ice harvesting. In 1866, four years after Thoreau's death, Ice Fort Cove was developed into an amusement park and picnic ground with its own railroad station.*

We've reached the westernmost limit of Walden Pond. Looking back east over the water offers the longest view of the lake. The distant Eastern Shore, which seemed so immense when we were there at our third stop, is instead a blur between two fuzzy horizontal lines. The top line is the horizon of the tree canopy. The bottom line is the shoreline between water and beach. Barely visible at the crosshairs of everything is the tiny dot of the massive two-story concrete bathhouse.

Behind us to the west are the tracks of the MBTA, the Massachusetts Bay Transportation Authority, locally known as "the T." This diesel-powered commuter railroad is the successor to the wood-fired multipurpose railroad of Thoreau's era. West of Ice Fort Cove, the Fitchburg Line services these stations: Concord, West Concord, South Acton, Littleton, Shirley, North Leominster, Fitchburg, and Wachusett. The current schedule has trains passing back and forth about thirty times per day. Many of the commuters are still fulfilling Thoreau's heartfelt wish that their days be brightened by momentary glimpses of the lake.

Henry also commuted by rail when he traveled between pond and village. But he walked, not rode, the rails. He had found a straight, clean shot between his family's house on Texas Street and his one-room house in the woods. The railway made for a well-drained, flat, broad, sunny, breezy, and private pathway that was free of the dust, commotion, manure, and gossip of local roads. Thoreau was explicit about his preference: "The railroad is perhaps our pleasantest and wildest road. It only makes deep cuts into and through the hills—on it are no houses nor foot travellers. The travel on it does not disturb me. The woods are left to hang over it."

Without going uphill or downhill, and without veering left or right, Thoreau could follow the railroad right of way through artificial canyons cut forty feet deep into soft glacial sediment, and out on to causeways piled high above wetlands and streams. The banks of these features, whether excavated above railroad grade or filled below it, were oozing with mud-flows and sprouting with weeds, creating a riot of ecological instability and change. For the climax of *Walden,* Thoreau called readers' attention to the delicate branching pattern produced by muddy rivulets flowing down the faces of the tallest excavation, known as the

## Views of Ice Fort Cove from Henry's window

"Thus for sixteen days I saw from my window a hundred men at work like busy husbandmen, with teams and horses and apparently all the implements of farming, such a picture as we see on the first page of the almanac; . . . and now they are all gone, and in thirty days more, probably, I shall look from the same window on the pure sea-green Walden water there, reflecting the clouds and the trees, and sending up its evaporations in solitude, and no traces will appear that a man has ever stood there."

The western window of Thoreau's house gave him a partial view of the industrial-scale ice-cutting operation that took place during his second winter (1846–1847). This was the only part of the pond he could see when sitting at his desk.

A locomotive steaming away from Concord above Ice Fort Cove during the early twentieth century. (Courtesy of the Thoreau Society, The Thoreau Society Archives at the Walden Woods Project's Thoreau Institute Library)

Deep Cut. For Thoreau, the similarity between the branching patterns of the miniature mudflows and the local foliage symbolized the vigor of nature's redemption over the soils of industry.

There was never an ice fort here. Our stop was named for an imagined ice fort from the *Walden* chapter "The Pond in Winter." During the late winter of 1846–1847, Thoreau watched a "hundred men of Hyperborean extraction," meaning Irish laborers, congregate in this cove each morning, each "armed with a double-pointed pike-staff." They had been recruited as common laborers by Boston capitalist Frederic Tudor to harvest a great quantity of ice that could be shipped by rail in smaller batches to Boston. There the ice would be loaded onto sailing ships, sent around the world, and sold at a profit to the "sweltering inhabitants of Charleston and New Orleans, of Madras and Bombay and Calcutta." During the "midst of a hard winter," and using "many car-loads of ungainly looking farming tools, sleds, ploughs, drill-barrows, turf-knives, spades, saws, rakes," the Irishmen cut up the sheet-like slab of lake ice into "cakes," each the size of a suitcase.

On one occasion, one worker slipped into the icy water and would probably have died of hypothermia had Thoreau not warmed him up in his snug house where the woodstove was hot with the burning of pitch pine stumps.

After cutting cakes of ice from the cove, the laborers stacked them one on top of another. Tudor's inventory loomed so high and wide that Thoreau

## Whirlygig beetles left tracks on the water.

"From a hilltop . . . You can even detect a water-bug (*Gyrinus*) ceaselessly progressing over the smooth surface a quarter of a mile off; for they furrow the water slightly, making a conspicuous ripple bounded by two diverging lines, but the skaters [a different insect] glide over it without rippling it perceptibly. When the surface is considerably agitated there are no skaters nor water-bugs on it, but apparently, in calm days, they leave their havens and adventurously glide forth from the shore by short impulses till they completely cover it."

Thoreau correctly assigned his "water-bug" to the genus *Gyrinus*. Today, this insect is commonly known as the whirlygig beetle because it whirls around on the water surface. What he called "skaters" are now called striders, a family known as the Gerridae. These are a kind of fly in the order Hemiptera. These two types of creatures are associated with Ice Fort Cove because both prefer perfectly still water. Ice Fort Cove is the quietest place on the pond with respect to the prevailing westerly winds.

imagined it to be an old fort. The slabs

formed the solid base of an obelisk designed to pierce the clouds. They stacked up the cakes thus in the open air in a pile thirty-five feet high on one side and six or seven rods square, putting hay between the outside layers to exclude the air . . . At first it looked like a vast blue fort or Valhalla; but when they began to tuck the coarse meadow hay into the crevices, and this became covered with rime and icicles, it looked like a venerable moss-grown and hoary ruin, built of azure-tinted marble.

## The nearby symphony of industrial-scale ice harvesting

"To speak literally, a hundred Irishmen, with Yankee overseers, came from Cambridge every day to get out the ice. They divided it into cakes by methods too well known to require description, and these, being sledded to the shore, were rapidly hauled off on to an ice platform, and raised by grappling irons and block and tackle, worked by horses, on to a stack, as surely as so many barrels of flour, and there placed evenly side by side, and row upon row, as if they formed the solid base of an obelisk designed to pierce the clouds."

For weeks, the silence of Ice Fort Cove was shattered by the noises of an ice quarry, including the clank of chains, the shouts of men, the sawing of ice, and the slamming of ice blocks against one another. The flaring shape of the cove and the cold winter air would have intensified and sharpened the sounds of this heavy work.

Walden Pond made the perfect ice quarry because it met three criteria: cold weather, pure water, and rail transport. Walden's quiet western basin allowed cold, still air to settle below the steep banks to freeze the ice deeply and clearly. Walden's water was exceptionally pure, being fed solely by rain, snow, and aquifer seepage. Last, the quiet cove was directly accessible to the tracks. Surprisingly, the colossal mass of ice cakes with a staggering volume estimated to be 300,000 cubic feet was never used. There, the "ice fort" melted

This southern view across Ice Fort Cove shows the calmness of the water and the stone remains of a former structure of unknown origin, likely associated with the Lake Walden amusement park.

slowly in place before disappearing completely two summers later.

Thoreau described the pond freezing thickly every year beginning in early December, creating a thick slab of ice.

> Every winter the liquid and trembling surface of the pond
> . . . becomes solid to the depth of a foot or a foot and a half,
> so that it will support the heaviest teams, and perchance the
> snow covers it to an equal depth, and it is not to be distin-
> guished from any level field.

Over the whole lake, thick ice became a rigid sheet that expanded and contracted noisily as the temperature changed. It also flexed upward and downward as the air pressure or water level rose and fell. These stresses caused cracking, a form of seismicity. The acoustic results of these ice-quakes varied, depending on how fast the cracks propagated and how much they were muffled by snow.

For Thoreau, renewal—especially the return of life to his landscape in spring—was a central theme in *Walden*. Renewal was most dramatic during the final breakup of the lake ice in late March and early April.

> Suddenly an influx of light filled my house . . . I looked out
> the window, and lo! where yesterday was cold gray ice there
> lay the transparent pond already calm and full of hope as in
> a summer evening, reflecting a summer evening sky in its
> bosom.

Except when a train clatters by, Ice Fort Cove remains a very quiet place today. This was not so for the thirty-six years between 1866 and 1902, when many sounds echoed among the trees: the squeals of children cavorting in the water; the blare of horns at the band pavilion; and the roar of baseball fans cheering a home run. That's when a large, private, for-profit amusement park and picnic ground called Lake Walden operated on both sides of the railroad tracks. Officially, this was the "Walden Lake Grove Excursion Park." Its opening in 1866 coincided with the reburial of Thoreau's body to a new family plot on Authors Ridge in Sleepy Hollow Cemetery, only four years after his 1862 death. Henry seems to have had a premonition that an amusement park might be coming. With *Walden* in press, his *Journal* described ladies with parasols and gentlemen with oars boating on the pond.

By the time the Lake Walden excursion park opened, the American Civil War was over, the nation was rapidly industrializing, and its urbanizing citizens were becoming wealthier. To escape the cities, especially in summer, residents of greater Boston increasingly sought recreation in scenic locales. Beautiful Lake Walden—made easily accessible by train—quickly became a favorite destination for travelers and locals alike.

Lake Walden's developer

---

## Red maple
### (*Acer rubrum*)

"Already, by the first of September, I had seen two or three small maples turned scarlet across the pond, beneath where the white stems of three aspens diverged, at the point of a promontory, next the water. Ah, many a tale their color told! And gradually from week to week the character of each tree came out, and it admired itself reflected in the smooth mirror of the lake. Each morning the manager of this gallery substituted some new picture, distinguished by more brilliant or harmonious coloring, for the old upon the walls."

Ice Fort Cove, being sheltered, would have been perfect habitat for the red maple, also known as the swamp maple. Red maple does best where other trees do not, hence its preference for the cold, wet conditions of swamps. Yet without competition, red maple is a very adaptable species and can be found in a variety of settings. Thoreau celebrated this tree for its striking crimson beauty in early autumn.

Entering the Walden Lake Grove Excursion Park above Ice Fort Cove. Swings are to the right and a floating bathhouse to the left. (Entrance gate at Walden amusement park, photograph [187-]. Courtesy of the Concord Free Public Library)

was Charles L. Heywood, a Fitchburg Railroad employee. He knew the community well, having been a Concord resident. His family owned property on the pond. Heywood's project was a clone of Harmony Grove in nearby Framingham, Massachusetts, where a railroad spur had been bringing summertime visitors to the shore of Farm Pond since 1850. On July 4, 1854, Thoreau went to Harmony Grove with William Lloyd Garrison to give a fiery abolitionist speech, "Slavery in Massachusetts." Had Henry lived another twelve years, he might have given a comparable speech at Lake Walden about the ethics of landscape conservation.

## Charles L. Heywood opened Lake Walden in 1866.

An employee of the Fitchburg Railroad, Charles Heywood was the brains behind Lake Walden, a gated picnic ground and amusement park that lasted thirty-six years (1866–1902). Heywood's family lineage in Concord traces back to the time of settlement in 1635. His family owned about a third of the Walden Pond shoreline. The Lake Walden development project above Ice Fort Cove expanded to include a variety of amusements, including a racetrack, a baseball field, a dance pavilion, and a podium for speakers. Remains of that facility can be seen on the west side of the cove today.

For his Lake Walden development, Heywood chose the word *lake* to market the size and purity of the water, and the word *grove* to market its still-sylvan state. Day-trippers came in droves. Logically, the initial attractions were water-related: swimming, boating, scenic camping, picnicking, and strolling. Lakeside trails were cut into the woods and decorated with benches spaced out along the way. There were swings and playgrounds above the water. Lake Walden became a profitable commercial enterprise, with its own railroad station, a ticketed entry gate, food concessions, bathhouses, boat rentals, a music pavilion, dance hall, and a podium for public speeches.

As the amusement park grew in popularity, the facilities spilled out of the cove. A pedestrian bridge was built over the tracks to reach the adjacent flat portions of the ancient delta plain. There, developers found space on firm, dry ground for a sprawling campground, a racetrack, and a baseball diamond. The outlines of some of these facilities can still be detected through the trees using the almost magical imaging technology known as LiDAR, an acronym for Light Detection and Ranging. Various groups rented the facilities for gatherings, especially religious revivals, which were then very popular across America. On summer days in the 1870s, up to thirty-five railroad cars per day were disgorging passengers to Walden's western shore. During one notable picnic, sixteen carloads of children, a headcount of 1,129, came out from the cities to enjoy the water, woods, and fresh air.

The Lake Walden amusement park was hugely popular. Before it was destroyed by fire in 1902, the park had been heavily booked for thirty-six years, an interval many times longer than Thoreau's residency at the pond. When Walden the amusement park was reaching tens of thousands, *Walden* the book was reaching very few. The carnival-like atmosphere at the pond's western end was far more popular than the philosophical atmosphere of Thoreau's House Site, scarcely a quarter mile away.

The tip of Ice Fort Cove is the farthest we'll get from the wooden ramp of the Visitor Center where we started. Every subsequent step we take will bring us physically closer to home. Our conceptual journey, however, still has a long way to go.

Leaving Ice Fort Cove, the Pond Path rises up a long, gentle stairway onto the flat surface of the ancient delta plain on which the nearby railroad tracks were laid (see photo on page 48). The path then trends in a southeasterly direction until it rounds the next headland. At that point, the trail will carry us southwesterly into the next cove. Our movements will be like those of a sailboat tacking southeast and then southwest to head south. The midpoint of the next cove will be our next stop.

## AT A GLANCE

**Object:** The former tip of Sandbank Cove was erased when megatons of earthen debris were dumped into the water to create a bed for the railroad. The resulting embankment is an unusually straight slope that Thoreau called the "railroad sandbank."

**Location:** GPS coordinates 42° 26' 13.44" N, 71° 20' 37.54" W, 167 ft. The stop is midway along the nearly straight stretch of shore between adjacent headlands. Where we're standing now was once open water in a much larger cove. We face out into the lake.

**Moment:** In June 1844, the Fitchburg Railroad opened for business in Concord, bringing the industrial age to what had been a sleepy river town. Thoreau's sojourn at Walden Pond began less than one year later.

Twenty years ago, Sandbank Cove had a narrow but unusually fine-grained sandy beach. The curved shoreline is a twentieth-century phenomenon.

**Fun Fact:** Henry Thoreau moved to Staten Island from early May to mid-December 1843 to be a private tutor for William Emerson's children. His absence coincides with the main burst of railroad construction near Walden.

**Nature:** The engineered face of the railroad sandbank during the 1840s, together with similar created surfaces, provided sunny new habitats for a rich variety of weedy flowering plants and opportunistic creatures.

# 12: SANDBANK COVE

## Sense of Place

*When Thoreau lived at the pond, he enjoyed watching and hearing the trains whiz by on a regular schedule. The locomotive and cars were plainly visible because the tracks lay above a tall bank of bare sand that had been dumped into the cove.*

On his original survey map of Walden Pond, Thoreau drew the waterline of Sandbank Cove with a straight edge, the only place he did so at the pond. That's because the shore there in 1846 was perfectly parallel to the straight railroad tracks for a distance of 253 feet. The engineers who resurveyed the railroad alignment in 1922 for the creation of Walden Pond State Reservation also used a straight edge.

## Henry's affinity for the railroad

"The Fitchburg Railroad touches the pond about a hundred rods south of where I dwell. I usually go to the village along its causeway, and am, as it were, related to society by this link. The men on the freight trains, who go over the whole length of the road, bow to me as to an old acquaintance, they pass me so often, and apparently they take me for an employee; and so I am."

Thoreau was deeply ambivalent about the railroad and what it symbolized. Negatives included the smoke, noise, demand for fuel wood, wildfires set by burning cinders, and, worst of all, the partial destruction of one of Walden's coves, Sandbank Cove. Positives were the regular schedule the train gave to his life, a sense of connection to the rest of the world, a corridor to walk home on, and easy access to the nation's best library at that time at Harvard College.

## A red fox cursed at Thoreau in the moonlight.

"Sometimes I heard the foxes as they ranged over the snow-crust, in moonlight nights, in search of a partridge or other game, barking raggedly and demoniacally like forest dogs, as if laboring with some anxiety, or seeking expression, struggling for light and to be dogs outright and run freely in the streets . . . Sometimes one came near to my window, attracted by my light, barked a vulpine curse at me, and then retreated."

The red fox (*Vulpes vulpes*) is one of the most charismatic and symbolic creatures in Thoreau's writing. The link between the red fox and Sandbank Cove comes from Thoreau's reports of foxes cruising the railroad corridor, where the disturbed habitat provided good opportunities for prey species. The fox diet consists mainly of small rodents, but foxes will eat virtually anything. Their senses of sight, sound, and smell are very acute. Foxes are social animals, usually living in family dens and traveling in pairs. They are highly intelligent, resourceful, and elusive, which accounts for their frequent presence in folklore.

What accounts for the long, straight line? The original triangular tip of the cove had been filled in with earthen debris in 1843 by Irish laborers who built the railroad.

Before construction, the tip of the originally triangular cove had ended in a deep wetland channel that had likely carried overflow from Walden Pond during early postglacial time. To keep the track alignment straight over this vicinity, railroad engineers had two choices. They could either build a bridge over the tip of the cove or fill it with debris. They chose the latter. Nathaniel Hawthorne apparently watched the process, writing that it was "a torment to see the great, high, ugly embankment of the rail-road, which is here protruding itself into the lake." Luckily, Thoreau was away from Concord at the time, having moved to Staten Island to become a private tutor for the children of William Emerson, Ralph Waldo's brother. Henry's longest stay away from his family (early May to mid-December 1843) coincided with railroad construction along Walden's shore.

During the nineteenth century, intentionally created land like that which filled part of Walden Pond was often called *made land*. In the twentieth century, such land was called *artificial fill* by the geologists tasked with mapping earth materials. In the twenty-first century, with the growing realization that human impact is pervasive at a planetary scale, it no longer makes sense to use the word *artificial* for human-made land. There's nothing artificial about wanting to keep a railroad straight and level, which is why the fill was brought in and the original tip of the cove erased.

When Henry returned from Staten Island and visited Walden Pond, he called the straight line at the head of the cove the "railroad sandbank." Though the cove's original tip was missing, he included the cove within his inventory of measured coves, perhaps because he remembered what the cove used to look like. During the past century, the original arrow-straight shoreline of the sandbank

The shore of Sandbank Cove is unusually straight. Above the lake are three flat surfaces: the bench exposed by low water, the Pond Path above the boulders, and the ancient delta plain the railroad was built on (behind upper fence).

## Sugar maple
*(Acer saccharum)*

"Early in May, the oaks, hickories, maples, and other trees, just putting out amidst the pine woods around the pond, imparted a brightness like sunshine to the landscape, especially in cloudy days, as if the sun were breaking through mists and shining faintly on the hillsides here and there."

The headlands on either side of Sandbank Cove were excellent habitat for the sugar maple. This majestic tree has distinctive, five-pointed leaves, a vertically furrowed trunk, and winged seeds. Maples occur with oaks, but do better on moister soils. Thoreau enjoyed maple syrup, but he also tapped other types of trees, especially birch.

has become broadly curved with fine-grained shoreline sand drifting into the previously sharp corners. In places, this sand has the texture of what one might find on a nice ocean beach.

The shape of the bank in an uphill–downhill direction has also changed greatly. Today the slope of the railroad embankment is fully vegetated, gently curved, and armored by a rip-rap of boulders and crushed traprock. In Thoreau's day, the slope of the bank was unvegetated, perfectly straight, and consisted almost entirely of light-colored sand. A "yellow sand heap" is how he described a comparable bank elsewhere along the corridor. At the top of his sandbank was a layer of gravel dumped to create a strong bed for the original wooden ties, or "sleepers," to lie in. Above those ties were iron rails, which carried passengers and freight over what had once been open water. The metaphorical *Machine in the Garden*—the title of an extraordinary book by Leo Marx—is exemplified by the machine of the locomotive in the garden of the lake.

Initially, Thoreau loved the railroad. Its "sandbank" was a bright beacon easily seen from his doorway. At least five times a day, he had a chance to watch and hear the cars whiz, squeak, and clatter over the tracks, and enjoy the locomotive's whistle, chug, and roar. Watching the comings and goings of the train became a pleasant and regular part of Thoreau's routine that united him with the rest of the globe. "I watch the passage of the morning cars with the same feeling that I do the rising of the sun, which is hardly more regular." The train also kept him from feeling alone: "Now that the cars are gone by and all the restless world with them, and the fishes in the pond no longer feel their rumbling, I am more alone than ever."

Only after Thoreau left the pond in 1847 did his animus for the railroad rise up like bile. The locomotives created noise pollution, drank water for steam, and burned trees for fuel. "That devilish Iron Horse, whose ear-rending neigh is heard throughout the town, has muddied the Boiling Spring with his foot, and he it is that has browsed off all the woods on Walden shore." The chronology here is critical. When Henry departed from Walden Pond in 1847, the shore was largely wooded. That changed in

Sugar maple (*Acer saccharum*). Bucket for collecting maple sap in late winter. Thoreau experimented with tapping various types of trees. (© John Tomaselli/Alamy)

less than a decade. By the time of his last draft of *Walden* in 1854, he was lamenting the nearly total clear-cutting of the shore. His *Walden* sojourn, his *Life in the Woods,* had taken place just in the nick of time.

The name Sandbank Cove is used in this guide. Pond historian Barksdale Maynard used the name "Railroad Bay" for what was left of this cove after its tip was erased, following the precedent of H. W. Gleason's "R.R. Bay." The official name used by Walden Pond State Reservation is "Long Cove," inherited from Percival Meigs, a twentieth-century pond enthusiast. After *Walden*'s publication, Thoreau once used the phrase "the long cove" to describe the length of the sandbank. But based on the geometric conventions for his 1846 survey, the original cove was broad, but not long. To avoid this contradiction, I avoid the official name.

Henry described only two short beaches in *Walden:* one at the Eastern Shore, the other unspecified. The latter was almost certainly the beach below his "railroad sandbank." With no vegetation to prevent erosion of the shore, and with nothing but fine sand for the waves to slosh on, a conspicuous sandy beach of pure, fine sand would have been inevitable. Today, that sandy beach is gone, replaced with an armored slope of crushed rock and boulders.

The exceptionally pure, clean, white, well-sorted, evenly textured, and inorganic fine sand hidden below the modern riprap is not present elsewhere on Walden's shore. Almost certainly

---

**The whistle and scream of the locomotive**

"The whistle of the locomotive penetrates my woods summer and winter, sounding like the scream of a hawk sailing over some farmer's yard, informing me that many restless city merchants are arriving within the circle of the town, or adventurous country traders from the other side."

Thoreau loved to link human sounds with animal sounds. At Sandbank Cove, the train whistle becomes a hawk's scream, announcing that commerce is alive and well.

it had been hauled in from some deep, trackside excavation that penetrated into the lower, water-rinsed deposits of glacial Lake Sudbury, likely the "Deep Cut."

Before leaving Sandbank Cove, let's look straight down the slope into the depths as we did at Bare Peak. In both places, the water deepens and turns greenish much more rapidly than elsewhere on the shore. This steepness at the midpoint

> ### Nathaniel Hawthorne complained in 1843.
>
> Hawthorne befriended Thoreau in 1842 when he arrived in town with his new wife, Sophia Peabody Hawthorne, to live in the Old Manse. In 1843, Nathaniel Hawthorne, then a largely unknown nineteenth-century American novelist, was greatly disturbed by the railroad construction activities at Sandbank Cove, which he thought ruined the view. The Hawthornes left Concord after a few years but moved back again in 1860.

of a cove indicates that fill has been added.

In 1928, this southwestern corner of Walden Pond became the final piece of lakeshore added to the public park. Without this final acquisition, private homes would almost certainly have been built on the headlands between the coves in the southwestern part of Walden Pond, making them visible from everywhere on the lake. The construction of private residential homes occurred at White Pond to the west, Walden's so-called twin. White Pond is a lovely place for a select few. Walden remains a lovely place for everyone.

There's only one more cove to go. Getting there requires leapfrogging over the next headland. Once there, we'll turn around and look back out toward the open lake.

## AT A GLANCE

**Object:** Deep Cove is the most perfectly shaped, sharply tipped, and isolated cove on the lake. The tip of this cove coincides with the groundwater boundary between inflow to and outflow from the pond.

**Location:** GPS coordinates 42° 26' 11.93" N, 71° 20' 24.69" W, 164 ft. Our target is where the fenced Pond Path makes its sharpest curve around the innermost recess of the cove. There, we'll look outward across the lake to Thoreau's Cove.

**Moment:** On August 1, 1955, Middlesex County Commissioner Brennan began a futile two-week experiment to lower the level of Walden Pond by pumping out 4,000 gallons per minute for twenty-four hours per day.

Deep Cove is so shallow that its upper portion was dry in May 2017. Note the small bar to the right of the cove. Thoreau's Cove is directly across this widest view of the lake.

**Fun Fact:** After two weeks, the pumping of approximately 80 million gallons of water caused the pond to drop only one foot. This amount of water is equivalent to 2 million bathtubs or 122 Olympic-sized swimming pools.

**Nature:** Deep Cove froze early in winter and thawed late in spring. It occupies a deeply shaded recess below a north-facing slope that provides habitat for shade-tolerant plants that cannot compete on the sunny north shore.

# 13: DEEP COVE

## Sense of Place

*Thoreau seldom visited Deep Cove, the most isolated and hidden cove on the lake. The tip of the cove, an important groundwater boundary, was the site of a failed experiment to pump the lake down to improve the swimming.*

In *Walden,* Thoreau writes of "the beautifully scalloped southern shore, where successive capes overlap each other and suggest unexplored coves between." The key word here is *unexplored.* Thoreau never explicitly mentions Deep Cove by any name. His apparent dearth of attention to this cove has to do with its location as the farthest point across the lake from his House Site. This cove also lies on the far side of the lake from Concord Center and is the one most removed from the town's two main transportation corridors, the railroad track to the west and Walden Street to the east.

### Henry's isolated cove

"The shore is irregular enough not to be monotonous. I have in my mind's eye ... the beautifully scalloped southern shore, where successive capes overlap each other and suggest unexplored coves between."

When seen from Thoreau's Waterfront, Deep Cove is the unexplored cove at the center of his scalloped southern shore. Thoreau used the word "deep" to describe this cove because it deeply indents the shore between headlands he called "capes." The shaded recess of Deep Cove conveyed a sense of mystery.

Although Deep Cove was relatively inaccessible for Thoreau, he still chose to begin his 1846 mapping project at its innermost point. He designated its tip as the first of thirteen alphabetically labeled survey stations. Beginning with "A" and ending with "M," he worked his way from unfamiliar to familiar territory.

## The American robin symbolized the arrival of spring.

"The change from storm and winter to serene and mild weather, from dark and sluggish hours to bright and elastic ones, is a memorable crisis which all things proclaim. It is seemingly instantaneous at last . . . I heard a robin in the distance, the first I had heard for many a thousand years, methought, whose note I shall not forget for many a thousand more—the same sweet and powerful song as of yore."

The central theme of *Walden* is renewal: of the day with morning, and of the year with the melting of the ice on the pond, which occurs at Deep Cove later than at the other coves. In this passage, Thoreau exults in the sound of the migratory American robin (*Turdus migratorius*) as a symbol of the life that returns with spring. This bird is a very abundant and highly visible member of the thrush family. It hunts for ground invertebrates such as worms. The robin prefers a mixed habitat of open fields and dense cover. Its predators are small carnivorous mammals and birds of prey.

Based on Henry's mapping, Deep Cove is the most perfectly shaped of all coves, a nearly perfect isosceles triangle when the water is at normal height. Surely, this is the "deep and triangular" cove of Thoreau's *Journal*. Here, "deep" refers to the depth of the recess in map view, not of the water in a vertical view. Deep Cove meets Thoreau's criteria for a true cove because it's quite shallow near the tip and has a bar where it fronts the western basin.

During the railroad construction in 1843, Deep Cove was reported to be the location of a small, ad hoc shantytown occupied by Irish workers and their families. The recent immigrants likely drew water from the lake and burned fires in front of their dugout shacks. Larger clusters of shanties lay closer to the tracks and closer to Concord, particularly near

American robin (*Turdus migratorius*).
For Thoreau, the American robin
symbolized the coming of spring.
(© William Leaman/Alamy)

the Deep Cut, where man-
ual labor was concentrated. In
*Walden*'s chapter "Economy,"
Thoreau described the shanty
he purchased from Mr. Collins
for its boards. Mrs. Collins showed him a

> peaked cottage roof, and not much else to be seen, the dirt
> being raised five feet all around as if it were a compost heap
> . . . Doorsill there was none . . . It was dark, and had a dirt
> floor for the most part, dank, clammy, and aguish [feverish],
> only here a board and there a board which would not bear
> removal.

Little evidence of these temporary towns remains, except for a
few small cellar holes and dugouts on the hillsides. These shallow
depressions remain barely distinguishable from those created by

## Thunder and lightning across the pond from Thoreau's house

"In one heavy thunder-shower the lightning struck a large pitch pine across the pond, making a very conspicuous and perfectly regular spiral groove from top to bottom, an inch or more deep, and four or five inches wide, as you would groove a walking-stick. I passed it again the other day, and was struck with awe on looking up and beholding that mark, now more distinct than ever, where a terrific and resistless bolt came down out of the harmless sky eight years ago."

Reading this passage invokes dramatic sounds from our memories: a sizzling crack of lightning, the resounding boom of its thunder, the tearing split of a falling tree, its crash to the ground, and then silence. Deep Cove is directly "across the pond" from "Thoreau's World," suggesting this was the vicinity he was describing.

trees blown down during powerful windstorms.

A fascinating but failed effort to manage public swimming at Walden Pond took place at Deep Cove beginning August 1, 1955. Heavy rains the previous year had flooded the Eastern Shore. Thousands of disappointed swimmers demanded that something be done. In response, Commissioner Thomas B. Brennan decided to pump water up from Walden Pond and send it down toward the Sudbury River. Deep Cove was the most logical place for a pumping station because it's the closest point of natural groundwater outflow relative to park headquarters. Brennan installed two giant, noisy, gasoline-powered sump pumps. Each had an intake hose submerged in Deep Cove and an outflow hose that rose up and over the low ridge to Heywood Meadow to the south. After two weeks of continuous pumping at a rate of 4,000 gallons per minute, the water level in Walden Pond dropped only one foot, bringing no improvement to the swimming.

Brennan's mistake was to think of Walden as a giant bathtub that holds a finite amount of water. But remember that the pond doesn't "hold" water in the traditional sense. Instead, it exposes, or makes visible, a portion of the invisible underground water stored in a much larger aquifer. Thoreau was correct in saying: "The pond was my well ready dug."

Pumping such a well in sand and gravel steepens the nearby groundwater gradients in all directions, creating what's known as a "cone of depression." For every gallon Brennan pumped out, nearly another gallon flowed back in. The shallow cone he created in the water table caused the water to flow into Walden from all sides, especially from the east. He wasn't pumping down a lake. He was pumping down the larger aquifer that feeds that lake.

Beginning March 13, 2010, record-breaking rainfall even heavier than Brennan's 1955 scenario raised Walden Pond and its surrounding aquifer. More than ten inches of rain fell within a span of three days, an amount not exceeded in the previous century. The result was a time-delayed rise in the stage of Walden Pond that flooded the beach and made Wyman Meadow a bay of the lake. This time, there was no attempt to pump the lake down. Instead, the management cut park attendance in half by cutting parking in half. This epoch of high water is when the bridge at Wyman Meadow was installed.

Thoreau emphasized to his readers that Walden Pond had neither inlet nor outlet streams. Hydrologists classify such water bodies as *flow-through* lakes or

## Ralph Waldo Emerson bought real estate in 1845.

The sage of Concord was also a dealer of real estate and a country squire. He bought nearly the whole of the south shore of Walden Pond on November 29, 1845, paying $30 per acre to Abel Moore for 41 acres. This purchase included all of Deep Cove, as well as a rocky overlook later known as Emerson's Cliff. Thoreau surveyed the entire parcel with a pocket compass. In his dotage, Emerson looked back on Henry as his dearest friend.

### Eastern hemlock
#### (*Tsuga canadensis*)

"He [Alek Therien] had soaked hemlock leaves in water and drank it, and thought that was better than water in warm weather."

Of all the coves at Walden, Deep Cove is the shadiest and coolest. Hemlock prefers these conditions for habitat, which explains why hemlock seedlings are common in this vicinity today. Thoreau described a mature hemlock as "standing like a pagoda in the midst of the woods." Alek was the Canadian woodchopper that Thoreau befriended, greatly admired, and wrote extensively about in *Walden*.

ponds, the main idea being that the water flows through them, not into or out of them. Nowhere else at the pond is this process more clear than at Deep Cove. Its southern tip marks an unseen groundwater boundary. On the cove's eastern shore, and everywhere farther east, water seeps into the pond from the aquifer. On its western shore, and everywhere farther to the west, water seeps away from the pond into the aquifer.

The view from Deep Cove across to Thoreau's Cove is the best place to reflect on Walden's water budget. There are only two critically important boundary surfaces. The first is the horizontal surface of the lake, Thoreau's "field of water." The other boundary is a vertical cross-section across the lake, an imaginary slice between the tip of Deep Cove and the tip of Thoreau's Cove. This slice is bounded by the flat line of the lake surface and the irregular line of the lake bottom.

For the horizontal boundary, the water budget is up and down via precipitation and evaporation, respectively. Rain and snow bring in about 45 percent of Walden's total water each year. Evaporation returns 26 percent of the total back to the atmosphere. Every droplet of drizzle and flake of snow is a gain to Walden's budget and every molecule of water that evaporates is a loss.

The vertical boundary has a water budget as well. Everywhere to the east, groundwater arrives via aquifer seepage flowing inward from all directions (except west). This inflow brings in 55 percent

Eastern hemlock (*Tsuga canadensis*). Seedling hemlocks are present on Walden's shaded south shore.

of the total annual gain. Everywhere to the west, groundwater escapes into the aquifer outward in all directions (except east). This outflow accounts for 74 percent of the total annual loss.

Keeping the pond in balance from top to bottom and from east to west requires something astonishing: a very slow but very steady current of water flowing from east to west through Walden's three basins.

Conceptually, Walden Pond's water budget behaves very much

View across Deep Cove toward its western shore at low water. Sandbank Cove is hidden to the left around the point. Ice Fort Cove is opposite to the right.

like the ice budget of the tiny glaciers found in cirques (bedrock hollows) below high mountain summits. Thoreau saw empty cirques on Mount Katahdin and Mount Washington when he climbed these high peaks. A cirque glacier appears motionless to the viewer, but there's actually a very slow, steady flow of ice through a midpoint called the *equilibrium line*. Something similar happens at Walden Pond, but instead of glacier ice, there is an invisible slow flow of water from east to west across an equilibrium line between Deep Cove and Thoreau's Cove.

"For four months in the year," Thoreau wrote of Walden Pond, "its water is as cold as it is pure at all times; and I think that it is then as good as any, if not the best, in the town." Like good wine, the water from this "deep and capacious spring" was carefully filtered and properly aged. The texture and composition of its aquifer— glacially crushed and rinsed granite—ensured that only the purest water seeped into the pond. Thoreau's mid-nineteenth-century rainfall and snowfall were also pure because they predated the ubiquitous air pollution associated with fossil fuels. Because Walden Pond holds so much water (about 850 million gallons), a water molecule remains in the lake, on average, about five years. Some molecules arrive and leave within minutes. Others may linger for centuries. A trace of Thoreau's water might be with us today.

So far, all three stops in this southwest sector have been inside the coves of "Walden's Star." Our next stop from an overlook will give us a chance to look back on them all.

To get there, we need to start walking away from the tip of Deep Cove along the Pond Path. Every step will broaden our view by revealing more of the large western basin. Our target destination is the exact place where the western basin is the widest but the eastern basin has not yet come into view. This will be just short of the next headland and just above a short stone stairway leading down to the water. That will be our penultimate stop.

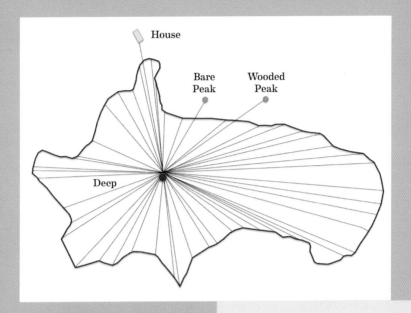

## AT A GLANCE

**Object:** As with the bridge at Wyman Meadow, the point of interest is not the place we stand but what we can see from that place. Here, our focus is on the radial symmetry of the pond over Walden's western basin.

**Location:** GPS coordinates 42° 26' 14.86" N, 71° 20' 23.07" W, 164 ft. The low overlook will be from the Pond Path above a stone stairway made of large slabs. At the correct place we can look through the trees to the center of the western basin without seeing the eastern basin.

**Moment:** On November 29, 1845, Ralph Waldo Emerson bought this land from Abel Moore for $30 per acre. The 41-acre parcel, his second purchase at Walden Pond, was then a woodlot extending down to the shore from a

To reduce the scale of his original survey map, Thoreau drew radial lines from the center above the deepest hole. This illustration matches the radial symmetry of the lake described in *Walden*.

rocky pinnacle later named Emerson's Cliff.

**Fun Fact:** Using a pocket compass, Thoreau surveyed Emerson's woodlot five years before he chose surveying as a vocation in 1850. On the back of his map are drawings of boat designs.

**Nature:** The flora in this shaded vicinity includes more hemlock, moss, and maple than on the opposite side, where oak and pine thrive on sunnier slopes.

# 14: OBSERVATORY

## Sense of Place

*From this elevated vista, the view across the lake brings the six stops of "Thoreau's World" into one scene (House Site, Waterfront, Thoreau's Cove, Bare Peak, Wyman Meadow, and Bean Field). This vista is the best view of Walden's star-shaped western basin.*

The Observatory gives us a chance to look back on Thoreau's little corner of the universe as one holistic place. Gazing in our direction from the opposite shore, he was inspired to write: "I have, as it were, my own sun and moon and stars, and a little world all to myself," a "forever new and unprofaned, part of the universe." There he also learned that solitude is not the same as loneliness: "Why should I feel lonely? Is not our planet in the Milky Way?"

Let's imagine pointing a telescope across the water and bringing "Thoreau's World" into focus. To the right on the horizon is Bare Peak, Thoreau's favored overlook

### Henry's astronomical allusion to his "little world"

"This whole earth which we inhabit is but a point in space . . . Why should I feel lonely? Is not our planet in the Milky Way?"

As Earth is to the Milky Way, so too is Walden Pond to the blue galaxy of kettle lakes that span the northern United States from the cranberry bogs of Nantucket Island to the alkaline prairie potholes of central Montana. In this astronomical allusion, Thoreau points out that loneliness is more about perception than distance. The Observatory provides our best view of "Thoreau's World."

## Red squirrels were Thoreau's whimsical friends.

"Usually the red squirrel (*Sciurus Hudsonius*) waked me in the dawn, coursing over the roof and up and down the sides of the house, as if sent out of the woods for this purpose. In the course of the winter I threw out half a bushel of ears of sweet corn, which had not got ripe, on to the snow-crust by my door, and was amused by watching the motions of the various animals which were baited by it . . . All day long the red squirrels came and went, and afforded me much entertainment by their manoeuvres. One would approach at first warily through the shrub oaks, running over the snow-crust by fits and starts like a leaf blown by the wind, . . . the little impudent fellow . . . a singularly frivolous and whimsical fellow."

Henry fed red squirrels (*Tamiasciurus hudsonicus*) all year long at his house so that he could watch their antics. In his day, they were known as pine squirrels to differentiate them from the gray squirrels more common in deciduous habitat. The pines of Thoreau's House Site are visible from the Observatory. Red squirrels responded particularly well to the corn he left for them because they live mainly on seeds, particularly those of pinecones, which are similar in size to seeds of corn. Their frenetic "manoeuvres" and chase scenes often involve males competing with each other for the chance to mate with estrous females.

The antics of the red squirrel (*Tamiasciurus hudsonicus*) greatly amused Thoreau. (Donna Dewhurst, courtesy of the U.S. Fish & Wildlife Service)

above Walden's bold northern shore. Below that high point to the west lies Thoreau's Cove, the largest shallow recess of the whole lake. That cove heats up to the temperature of tepid bathwater in August and freezes like a pane of glass in early winter. On the western shore of that cove is land formerly owned by Cyrus Hubbard that Henry used as his Waterfront. Above and behind that shore is a south-facing hollow containing Thoreau's House Site. Slightly behind the House Site, the horizon levels off above the ancient delta plain that held Henry's Bean Field. Just this side of that flat surface is a hole in the forest canopy, below which lies Wyman Meadow, where Henry went fishing in a temporarily flooded part of the lake. These six stops can be likened to six planets facing a giant star composed of pure water.

## The splashing and raucous quacking of ducks

"For hours, in fall days, I watched the ducks cunningly tack and veer and hold the middle of the pond, far from the sportsman . . . When compelled to rise they would sometimes circle round and round and over the pond at a considerable height . . . but what beside safety they got by sailing in the middle of Walden I do not know, unless they love its water for the same reason that I do."

Ducks used the middle of the pond for safety's sake. Thoreau sought the middle for symmetry's sake. This center is best seen from the Observatory. On the water, ducks splash and quack. In the air, the sounds are mainly associated with flight.

Let's rewind back to 1845–1847, when Henry Thoreau was doing his thing on the other side of the lake. Using our telescope, we see him launch his boat at the Waterfront and row straight across toward where we stand. Soon, we begin to hear the pull of his oars and the rhythmic gush of his wake. Midway across, he lets the boat glide over the deepest part of the pond. Then, using his stone-on-a-string, he fathoms the depth to 102 feet, the deepest point in Massachusetts.

From the middle of the lake, he noticed that most shoreline distances were comparable. He called this discovery the "rule of the two diameters."

Having noticed that the number indicating the greatest depth was apparently in the center of the map, I laid a rule on the map lengthwise, and then breadthwise, and found, to my surprise, that the line of greatest length intersected the line of greatest breadth exactly at the point of greatest depth . . .

At that central point, Thoreau occupied the epicenter of his local universe. Being "full of light and reflections," his lake "becomes a lower heaven itself," where the pull of gravity seems to have disappeared: "In such transparent and seemingly bottomless water, reflecting the clouds," he wrote, "I seemed to be floating through the air as in a balloon." While watching a school of perch, "their swimming impressed me as a kind of flight or hovering, as if they were a compact flock of birds passing just beneath my level on the right or left, their fins, like sails, set all around them."

Beneath that central point, his deep lake was covered with a uniformly thick layer of warm, wind-mixed water about twenty feet thick. The warm layer floated above a deeper mass of much colder, motionless water. In winter, a uniformly thick layer of snow and ice floated there instead. At such times, Thoreau walked on water—albeit in solid, crystal-

White pine (*Pinus strobus*) was arguably Thoreau's all-time favorite tree.

line form. Peering down through a chopped hole in the ice and looking into the liquid beneath made him realize that "Heaven is under our feet as well as over our heads."

Let's now shift seasons from the frozen winter to a lovely warm summer day. Thoreau is still in the center of the pond, but is drifting lazily in his rowboat. Under a dome of blue sky, his gaze encompasses the encircling wooded shores.

> The forest has never so good a setting, nor is so distinctly beautiful, as when seen from the middle of a small lake amid hills which rise from the water's edge . . . The trees have ample room to expand on the water side, and each sends forth its most vigorous branch in that direction.

Thoreau had many other experiences from the center of this star-shaped lake, translating them into the prose-poetry of *Walden.* On one occasion, a solitary loon lured him there to play hide and seek, diving into water nearly a hundred feet down. On a different day, and watching the center from the shore, he noticed that "when the sun arose, mists, like ghosts," withdrew "stealthily . . . in every direction into the woods." As the sun climbed, gentle currents of air were being drawn outward from the center by the greater warmth

## White pine
### (*Pinus strobus*)

"Near the end of March, 1845, I borrowed an axe and went down to the woods by Walden Pond, nearest to where I intended to build my house, and began to cut down some tall, arrowy white pines, still in their youth, for timber."

The old-growth white pines of New England were so lofty, majestic, tall, and straight that they were reserved for ships' masts. Much white pine was cut down in Thoreau's era, but pines have since regrown as colonizers of abandoned fields and pastures. In April 1859, Thoreau labored for Emerson to plant four hundred white pines on his former House Site and Bean Field.

### Bronson Alcott philosophized until 1888.

Originally from Connecticut, Bronson Alcott was Thoreau's philosophical soul mate for longer than anyone. After meeting Thoreau in the late 1830s, he helped the younger man raise his house in 1845, praised *Walden* in 1854, eulogized Thoreau's 1862 death with a tribute titled "The Forester," inaugurated his memorial cairn in 1872, and promoted Thoreau's legacy until 1888. Bronson Alcott was the longest-lived member of the original transcendentalist community. Alcott, a philosopher, is linked to our most philosophical stop, the Observatory.

of the dark wooded land relative to the brightly reflective cool water. On midsummer mornings, Thoreau rowed out to that center to let these radial breezes, called *zephyrs,* decide what shore he was destined to visit.

I have spent many an hour, when I was younger, floating over its surface as the zephyr willed, having paddled my boat to the middle, and lying on my back across the seats, in a summer forenoon, dreaming awake, until I was aroused by the boat touching the sand, and I arose to see what shore my fates had impelled me to; days when idleness was the most attractive and productive industry.

From the center of the lake one evening Thoreau heard echoes return with a "circling and dilating sound," amplified by the steep, tree-banked shores as if he were inside a drum. Each wave of sound "elicited a growl from every wooded vale and hillside."

Boating to Walden's center brought Thoreau above the pond's "deepest resort," his closest approach to "God and Heaven." Here, the glacial meltdown had been most intense, creating Walden's deepest hole. Surrounding that hole are concentric landscape rings rising up from the lake bottom to the shore, and up from the shore to the flat delta plain.

Finally, the center of the lake is an ideal place to visualize how Walden works as a single, colossal, organic machine with starlike radial symmetry. Four material realms work together: the central lake of water exposed at the bottom of the kettle basin; the central pocket of air resting above the water within that same basin; the land surrounding the air; and the aquifer surrounding the lake. These four realms function like the instruments in a quartet that never stops playing.

New England is widely known for its four distinct seasons. Walden Pond puts on a spectacular display. Its tall, steep banks create a theater in the round, enhancing the parade of seasonal colors seen by regular visitors twice as often in summer as in fall, in fall as in spring, and in spring as in winter. The same ranking—summer, fall, spring, winter—applies to first-time visitors, most of whom arrive from far away.

The Observatory is a great place to watch the seasonal parade of "Thoreau's World."

Early spring is blustery, with sere

Cross section of Walden's organic machine (system) shows the four realms (lake, air, aquifer, and land) meeting at the shore. Each realm exchanges matter and energy with two others.

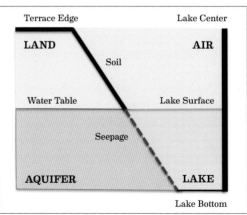

gray hillsides, occasional snow flurries, and gusty winds. The soils are sodden with moisture. By day the frozen ground melts, causing bare soils to ooze downward in rivulets of flowing sand and silt. Soaking rains warm the soil by thawing the last of the frozen ground. Over the pond, what had been white snow becomes gray slush, which freezes at night. The gray ice breaks into slabs that shift like tectonic plates. "The ice in the pond at length begins to be honeycombed, and I can set my heel in it as I walk." And then, miraculously, one night the ice is replaced by clear and rippling blue water. Birds migrate northward. The land greens with "the first tender signs of the infant year just peeping forth with the stately beauty of the withered vegetation which had withstood the winter."

Late spring brings lushness and a frenzy of mating. The banks above the pond become darker green in every direction. Birdsong radiates from every flowering bush. Insects buzz, frogs croak, and turtles come out of their slumber. Skunks prowl. The fragrance of flowers perfumes the air.

> Early in May, the oaks, hickories, maples, and other trees, just putting out amidst the pine woods around the pond, imparted a brightness like sunshine to the landscape, especially in cloudy days, as if the sun were breaking through mists and shining faintly on the hillsides here and there.

Early summer brings heat. Thoreau's beans ripen, along with berries and annual flowers. The sumacs outside of Thoreau's house grow so fast they snap and fall to the ground with a whoosh. Swimming, then called "bathing," becomes a daily routine. Thunderstorms roll in unexpectedly. "There came up a shower, which compelled me to stand half an hour under a pine, piling boughs over my head, and wearing my handkerchief for a shed." Thoreau drinks from cold groundwater springs or from a bucket drawn up from the deep lake.

Late summer brings drought and the panting heat of dog days. Dusty ground, super-humid air, blood-red sunsets, and the ripening and rotting smells of fruits and berries, domestic and wild.

Early fall blows in on the northwest wind. The air clears. Farmers lay in their stores. The land readies itself for frost. The autumnal tints arrived earlier at Walden then than they do now.

> Already, by the first of September, I had seen two or three small maples turned scarlet across the pond . . . And gradually from week to week the character of each tree came out, and it admired itself reflected in the smooth mirror of the lake. Each morning the manager of this gallery substituted some new picture, distinguished by more brilliant or harmonious coloring, for the old upon the walls.

Brisker winds add oxygen to the water. Reduced sunlight quells plankton growth. Walden becomes blue-green as its water reaches peak clarity.

> In such a day, in September or October, Walden is a perfect forest mirror, set round with stones as precious to my eye as if fewer or rarer . . . It is a mirror which no stone can crack, whose quicksilver will never wear off.

Late fall turns the land russet. Leafless stems and buds, gray-brown with a touch of dark purple, lock up for the year. Gray skies spit snow. Nearby ponds glaze over with thin black ice. The ancient delta plain appears through the twigs like a high flat rim on every part of the shore, stretching "away toward the prairies of the West."

In early winter, Thoreau drags stumps and deadfall branches back to his yard, where he chops and spits firewood and stacks it in his shed. Genuine cold sets in when the north wind blows. Walden begins to freeze, being "skimmed over in the shadiest and shallowest coves, some days or even weeks before the general freezing." The bulk of Walden, however, remains liquid, given the enormous quantity of heat stored in its hundreds of millions of gallons of summer-warmed water. Then, during one clear, quiet, starry night, the entire lake surface turns solid. What had been a liquid forest mirror becomes a sheet of frosted glass.

Dry snowfalls drift over the glaze of fresh ice in white waves. One heavy snow is all that's needed to make the pond indistinguishable from a nearby level field. Old Man Winter drops by Thoreau's house to keep him company.

The fishermen wade through snow down to the frozen lake to chop holes in the ice, catch iridescent green pickerel, and lay them down on the snow to freeze stiff. The winter sunlight weakens; the pond ice thickens. Changes in air temperature and pressure make ice-quakes the default background noise. By solstice time, the thick icy crust seems more alive than anything else. Gradually the sun rises higher in February, March, and April. The "frost comes out of the ground," the ice melts on the pond, and a rush of new life begins.

The seasonal cycle of Walden, captured so well in *Walden,* is ready to repeat itself once again.

At this point, we're all done with the places that inspired Thoreau's remarkable book. We've seen where he lived, followed his paths, and learned why *Walden* mirrors Walden. Now we have only one more stop to go—a place where we can hold Henry's nineteenth-century world of symmetry and purity in our left hand, and our twenty-first-century world of sprawling modernity in our right hand. Such a place lies only a few hundred feet ahead.

Thoreau found beauty everywhere. Sand ripples at Walden are most common in coves below eroded banks.

# SOUTHEAST: RE-ENTRY

With each step away from the Observatory, the radial symmetry of "Thoreau's World" distorts into an oblong shape crudely resembling a human footprint walking westward. The round heel of a right foot occupies the eastern basin, the curved arch narrows over the central basin, and the sole spreads out over the large western basin. Four toes, spread at odd angles, are the coves.

If the water is low enough, we'll take one of the stone stairways down to the water's edge and start walking around the broad curve of the southern shore. If the water's high, we'll just stay on the Pond Path. We're looking for the best view. If the boat launch comes into view from the east, we've gone just a bit too far. The goal is to find just the right spot where the western and eastern basins of Walden Pond are in balance and the central basin is straight ahead.

## AT A GLANCE

**Object:** The entire lake is our object of interest. From nowhere else can we see more of the lake. Panorama also offers the best place to compare Thoreau's historic landscape with our modern one.

**Location:** GPS coordinates 42° 26' 17.36" N, 71° 20' 18.39" W, 163 ft. Heading away from the Observatory, we will round the curve of the southern shore on the Pond Path looking for the northernmost viewpoint. If the gravel shoreline can be walked, it provides an even better view.

**Moment:** On June 5, 1995, the Walden Woods Project's Thoreau Institute held its grand opening. The institute is located in Lincoln, about a half-mile east of Walden Pond. In attendance were President Bill Clinton and First Lady Hillary Clinton.

The best view of Walden Pond is from the bank to the left and looking north to the right. This puts Walden's two largest basins on opposite sides.

**Fun Fact:** Panorama lies directly across the narrowest part of the main lake and faces the highest peak on the northern shore, one Thoreau called "Wooded Peak."

**Nature:** Along the shoreline curve of Panorama, the groundwater flows at right angles to the waterline with the shape of a fan. Nowhere else at Walden Pond is the flow pattern so simple and symmetric.

# 15: PANORAMA

## Sense of Place

*Panorama offers the best view of Walden Pond by putting the pond's western and eastern basins to left and right. This stop is also the best place to compare Thoreau's nineteenth-century landscape to the west with our twenty-first-century landscape to the east.*

There may be two longest views of Walden Pond, but there is only one *best* view: a continuous panoramic sweep from southwest to southeast. Appropriately, this view is from our final stop, Panorama, located at the northernmost point of the south shore. The lake seems largest here because it widens to the left and right over the western and eastern basins.

Nowhere else on the lake are we in a better position to ponder how Walden has changed through time. To the left is the westerly world of those who came via the railroad corridor: hundreds of Irish laborers (and their

> ### Henry's broadest view
>
> "White Pond and Walden are great crystals on the surface of the earth, Lakes of Light. If they were permanently congealed, and small enough to be clutched, they would, perchance, be carried off by slaves, like precious stones, to adorn the heads of emperors ... [but] ... They are too pure to have a market value."
>
> The most expansive, or lakelike, view of Walden Pond is to be found at Panorama. Happily, this "lake of light" is now held in the public trust within Walden Pond State Reservation, whereas its twin, White Pond, is privately owned.

families) laying the track; Henry David Thoreau walking the right-of-way; and thousands of visitors to the Lake Walden amusement park riding the rails in cars. To the right is the easterly world of those who came via automobile on Walden Street, beginning with the first horseless carriage at the dawn of the twentieth century, and continuing through the countless bicentennial busloads of school children coming to learn while having fun.

Panorama is also the best place on the pond to consider what naturalist Edwin Way Teale called the Walden "paradox," which is nicely captured in a pair of adjacent sentences from the opening lines of the "Management Principles and Goals" used by park authorities to manage this threatened property.

> Walden Pond State Reservation is an internationally acclaimed National Historic Landmark due to its association with Henry David Thoreau and his profoundly influential work *Walden; or, Life in the Woods.* Simultaneously, the reservation is a heavily visited recreation facility as it provides a diverse set of recreational activities, including high demand water-based activities.

In short, Walden Pond presents a management tradeoff between being conserved as an international cultural icon and being developed as a local swimming hole for residents of Greater Boston. This dilemma is reflected in the very name of the responsible organization: the Department of Conservation and Recreation.

Local and international visitors are motivated to visit the park for opposite reasons, and each group treks to an opposite sector of the pond. This we learned in 2013 based on statistics from a voluntary user-survey of pond visitors. When in-state residents were asked to identify their reason (or reasons) for visiting, nearly 89 percent reported they came to swim or use the beach, 32 percent to walk in the woods, and 10 percent to experience the world of Henry Thoreau. These statistics are flipped for out-of-state residents, with 85 percent coming because of Thoreau, 54 percent to walk in the woods, and only 35 percent to swim and walk the beach.

This geography of usage is clearly visible from Panorama. In-state visitors opt for the northeast sector to our right, where the Eastern Shore stop is the main draw. Out-of-state visitors opt for the northwest sector to our left, where the House Site stop is the main attraction.

This makes Panorama an ideal place for then-and-now comparisons. Broadly speaking, the Walden Pond of Thoreau's *then* is much the same as our *now:* a largely undeveloped body of fresh water in the woods a mile and a quarter south of America's oldest inland town. During prehistory, Walden Pond experienced limited use by Native Americans. During most of Euro-American history, the pond was mainly a local fishing hole with little value for potable water, housing, or agriculture. Walden's general

## The human animal manifested as a French Canadian woodchopper

"In him the animal man chiefly was developed. In physical endurance and contentment he was cousin to the pine and the rock. I asked him once if he was not sometimes tired at night, after working all day; and he answered, with a sincere and serious look, 'Gorrappit, I never was tired in my life.' But the intellectual and what is called spiritual man in him were slumbering as in an infant."

Thoreau was fascinated with a woodchopper named Alek Therien as a representative type of the human species (*Homo sapiens*), a more "animal" man than a spiritual or intellectual man. This immigrant French Canadian lumberman chopped alone all day without getting tired or lonely, and he always seemed happy whenever Thoreau stopped to visit. Henry envied Alek's completely original and simple life in the woods, as something Thoreau himself could never achieve. This woodchopper also taught him that "there might be men of genius in the lowest grades of life, however permanently humble and illiterate." The Panorama stop offers our broadest view of all types of human behavior.

lack of utility made it an "outback" with an aesthetic remoteness that would attract the transcendentalists, beginning in the 1830s.

By and large, we can still see, hear, and feel what Thoreau experienced: the depth, symmetry, and unity of the western basin have changed very little. At closer inspection, however, our Walden differs from Henry's in many ways.

When Thoreau lived at Walden from 1845 to 1847, the shoreline was heavily wooded, even though trees had been cut continuously in patches for more than two centuries. Following his departure, however, the woods were rapidly thinned in some places and clearcut in others to feed new sawmills associated with the railroad and the firewood boilers of locomotives, each a hungry iron horse. The sound of the axe was relentless in all directions. By the time of *Walden*'s 1854 publication, Thoreau was lamenting the loss of the woods that had inspired his book's subtitle only seven years earlier:

> But since I left those shores the woodchoppers have still further laid them waste, and now for many a year there will be no more rambling through the aisles of the wood . . . My Muse may be excused if she is silent henceforth. How can you expect the birds to sing when their groves are cut down?

By the time of Henry's death in 1862, only eight years later, Walden's banks had been nearly denuded of trees.

Despite all of the changes he saw, Thoreau decided that Walden Pond was unusually resilient to human onslaught. It survived.

> Though the woodchoppers have laid bare first this shore and then that, and the Irish have built their sties by it, and the railroad has infringed on its border, and the ice-men have skimmed it once, it is itself unchanged, the same water which my youthful eyes fell on; all the change is in me.

Even before Thoreau's death, the earlier clearings were growing back one patch at a time. The trees of today generally date from the decades of the 1860s to the 1890s, when the arrival of coal for space heating, and then petroleum, curtailed the previously insatiable demand for firewood. Without question, the trees of Walden Woods are now thicker, denser, and taller than they were during Thoreau's era. Sadly, they are missing the magnificent American chestnut, which became locally extinct in the early 1900s after an invasive fungus was accidentally introduced.

Walden's water quality has not held up as robustly as its woodland ecology. The lake now is seriously compromised relative to the purity of Tho-

## The sweet and melodious mooing of the milk cow

"At evening, the distant lowing of some cow in the horizon beyond the woods sounded sweet and melodious, and at first I would mistake it for the voices of certain minstrels by whom I was sometimes serenaded, who might be straying over hill and dale; but soon I was not unpleasantly disappointed when it was prolonged into the cheap and natural music of the cow. I do not mean to be satirical, but to express my appreciation of those youths' singing, when I state that I perceived clearly that it was akin to the music of the cow, and they were at length one articulation of Nature."

Panorama links the human music of a youthful chorus with the animal music of a cow lowing. This comparison jives with the focus of this stop, the comparing and contrasting of the sounds of Thoreau's world and ours. We all too easily forget that sounds are part of history.

reau's then. He described it as "so transparent that the bottom can easily be discerned at the depth of twenty-five or thirty feet." This visibility has since been halved to about fifteen feet. The water is still very clear by national standards, but lacks the remarkable purity that made Walden world famous. The chief concern is a higher concentration of plankton caused by an increase in biological nutrient being excreted from human beings. The second largest source of phosphorous nutrient is pollen, mainly from pine, the yellow dust

Wild grape (*Vitis riparia*). When ripe in later summer, Thoreau boated beneath their vines and feasted. (© F. Schussler/PhotoLink/Photodisc/Getty Images)

that arrives in early summer.

Another water quality difference involves invisible pollution that drifts in from the atmosphere. This includes global dust, automobile exhaust from busy local roads, and toxins from faraway incinerators and coal-burning power plants. Within the muck are radioactive isotopes from atomic bomb testing that peaked in the early 1960s. The water was more radioactive in that decade than now. During Thoreau's residency, the pond was his main source of potable water, and fish from the pond were important in his diet. Today people seldom drink the water or eat the fish for fear of contamination.

## Wild grape
### (*Vitis riparia*)

"When I first paddled a boat on Walden, it was completely surrounded by thick and lofty pine and oak woods, and in some of its coves grape-vines had run over the trees next the water and formed bowers under which a boat could pass."

Thoreau greatly enjoyed harvesting boatloads of wild grapes in early autumn, especially enjoying their intoxicating fermenting scent. Most common was the wild grape, also known as fox or riverbank grape. The world-famous, dark purple Concord grape was artificially bred and cultivated from wild varieties such as those that Thoreau collected. The link between wild and tame is a theme we explore at Panorama.

The shoreline has also changed greatly between Thoreau's then and our now. In his day, he found a steep, narrow, "stony shore" with "one or two short sandy beaches" and a perimeter that could be walked only during prolonged drought. Nowadays, under normal or low water stage, there is an extensive bench of dry sand and gravel around the pond perimeter. Thoreau's perimeter "belt of smooth rounded white stones like paving stones" is nowhere to be found, perhaps because most have been tossed into the water or skidded out onto the ice. The driftwood he described is nearly gone as well. During my regular teaching visits during the decade 2004 to 2014, the bench was mainly submerged. Within the last few years however, it is more often exposed than not, revealing what is essentially

## Edith Emerson Forbes donated land in 1922.

Edith Emerson Forbes (1841–1929) deserves public gratitude. Joined by other families, Edith led the effort to donate eighty acres of land to the public in May 1922. That generous donation created Walden Pond State Reservation, which now holds the entire pond perimeter in the public trust. This perimeter is best seen from the Panorama stop. Without Edith's effort, Walden Pond would probably look like many private lakeshore housing developments of today.

a century's worth of sediment pollution.

Back then, Thoreau experienced cold winters lasting from mid-December to late March, with thick snowfalls, and thick ice on the pond. He compared the freeze-up of the pond to the hibernation of a woodchuck that "closes its eyelids and becomes dormant for three months or more." He also compared his thick floes of lake ice to the marine pack ice of the Arctic. Now, winter at Walden is a significant season mainly during the months of January and February. Though cold snaps can still be dramatic, average winter minimum temperatures have risen steadily. The lake freezes later and less thickly than before. Warning signs are posted for thin ice. Scientists attempting to replicate Thoreau's measurements of ice thickness and water temperature dare not tread on the thin ice. Each year, fewer and fewer visitors witness a frozen pond.

Differences in the thickness of ice and the timing of freezing and thawing are due to the natural warming of the planet since Thoreau's era, amplified by anthropogenic warming of New England since the mid-1980s. In this region, the average annual temperature has been rising at twice the global average, with winter minimum temperatures rising fastest of all. Curiously, Thoreau was much more fearful about climate change in the opposite direction, a global cooling pushing us toward another glaciation.

The overall terrestrial ecology of now is fairly representative of what Thoreau saw then, though there are noticeable changes. While the woody vegetation remains mainly pine and oak adapted to excessively well-drained soils, recent ecological research reveals significant changes for flowers and shrubs. Approximately one-third of the species being studied have gone locally extinct. Flowering plants bloom about two weeks earlier than during Thoreau's time. Similarly, trees and shrubs leaf out on average two weeks earlier. These botanical changes are a direct consequence of climate change. The terrestrial animals are responding as well. Fewer birds are migrating, and their flight schedules are earlier in the spring and later in the fall. The timings of nesting and hatching have changed as well. These interpretations are based on Thoreau's excellent recordkeeping during the last decade of his life.

Before the 1960s, the pond was famous mainly for the literary, philosophical, and political content of *Walden.* Since then, Walden has become more widely known as the fountainhead of America's environmental movement, which emerged out of the conservation ethos of the 1940s and 1950s. After this transition, Thoreau was rightly claimed as "'*the* environmental prophet,' 'the founding father of environmental thought in America,' and the 'patron saint of American Environmental writing.'" More recently, he's being universally celebrated for living simply: "a man is rich in proportion to the number of things which he can afford to let alone."

Finally, Panorama offers a great place to think about the then and now of tourist sociology. Prior to the coming of the railroad, pond visitors were almost entirely the descendants of colonial English who settled eastern Massachusetts beginning in 1620. Related to these New Englanders was a small community of African Americans during the decades following the American Revolution. In 1843 an influx of Irish immigrants came to work on the railroad. They lived with their families in shantytowns along Walden's western edge. Yet to come were the later and greater waves of immigration from southern Europe associated with urban factory labor, and from northern Europe associated with the Homestead Act of 1862. Beginning in 1866, hordes of urban residents, including many of these immigrants, began day-tripping to Lake Walden by train.

Beginning in 1902, the automobile brought an even greater mix of visitor backgrounds and interests, though some racial and ethnic groups were discouraged. Today, pond attendance is multinational, multiethnic, and colorblind. Women no longer need to be escorted by men. Times have changed. But the central Walden experience has not.

That's it! Let's take a final look at the best view of Walden and start to walk back to the Visitor Center. Following the broad curve of the shore will gradually steer us slightly southward into the eastern basin. Marking the southern edge of that basin is a boat launch that was converted from the gravel quarry that operated there sporadically during the twentieth century.

Many of the stones in the walls near the boat launch are very different from the rounded, glacially milled boulders we saw at our fourth stop, Boulder Wall (see page 75). Much of the nearby hardscape was built with slabs of weathered fieldstone that were hauled down to the pond from abandoned upland farms. When Walden's original hardscape was built during the 1940s, the old farmstead stone walls were considered to be ordinary and plentiful sources of building material. Times have changed. Today fieldstone walls are awarded protection and are cherished as cultural artifacts and folk art. Prophetically, Henry Thoreau asked that old fieldstone walls be preserved as part of the aesthetic landscape. Now they are.

From the boat launch, the final leg of our tour will be a northward walk through the engineered landscape of the Eastern Shore. Eventually, we'll reach the bottom of the concrete E-Ramp that leads

back up to our second stop, the Terrace Edge. As we climb the ramp, we'll be leaving behind the colossal depression we've spent most of our tour within.

Much of the lichen-covered stone wall built along the Eastern Shore is composed of imported agricultural fieldstone.

When we reach the sidewalk, we will have returned to the larger, flatter, and busier world of the ancient delta plain that surrounds Walden Pond, and on which the nearby highways were built.

Pushing the button at the crosswalk to activate the flashing lights and the buzzing sounds will signal our return back to modern life. After walking across the road and glancing left toward our first stop, Simple House, we'll turn right onto the stone dust walkway. Reaching the base of the wooden ramp, we'll proceed up to the tall glass doors of the Visitor Center, where we began our tour together.

This unusual view looks back across the central basin to Deep Cove over a layer of thin ice. A circle of water welled up and refroze, signifying holism and change.

# LOOKING BACK

For many visitors, Walden Pond is a casual stroll around a pleasant lake in order to appreciate the trees, flowers, animals, and birds of the woodland landscape, perhaps with a stop at Henry's House Site. Our journey has been much more deliberate, a stop-and-go learning experience linking passages from *Walden* to the places that inspired those passages.

During our counterclockwise tour on the Pond Path, we sequenced our stops in geographic order. But now that we've experienced all fifteen stops, we can sequence their stories in historical order. The result can be a personalized history of Walden Pond based on actual experience.

Four of our stops conveyed the creation story of Walden Pond prior to human settlement. Thoreau told this story as the mythology of the "old settler and original proprietor, who is reported to have dug Walden Pond, and stoned it . . ." and who tells "stories of old time and of new eternity." Here, Henry is referring to the immense ice sheet responsible for creating the pond. The old settler's partner is Mother Nature, "a ruddy and lusty old dame, who delights in all weathers and seasons, and is likely to outlive all her children yet . . . an elderly dame . . . invisible to most persons, . . . [with] . . . a genius of unequalled fertility, and her memory runs back farther than mythology." Here, Henry is referring to the rebirth and organic redemption of living nature from that inhospitable ice-age world.

Boulder Wall became our time machine for traveling back to the origin of planet Earth, and to the tectonic origin of the land named New England by John Smith, a Puritan settler contemporaneous with those who settled Concord. Solid crystalline rock, similar in hardness to the boulders we saw stacked in the wall, supports everything in our world with a strong foundation, including Walden Pond. From such rock came everything we enjoy and depend on. Rock is the father and mother of us all. Or, as the poet James Merrill put it, the marriage of Father Time and Mother Earth was "on the rocks."

The moraine ridge of Bare Peak showed us where the ragged edge of the ice sheet paused on its way back to Canada. That was about 16,000 years ago, when the glacier was dying downward and receding northward, and was fronted by a broad glacial lake. During that pause, a staggering amount of meltwater sediment gushed out from beneath the glacier to bury masses of stagnant ice beneath where

Walden is today. Over time, that sediment built upward into the vast delta plain we encountered at four stops: Simple House, Terrace Edge, Bean Field, and south of Ice Fort Cove. Only later did the buried ice melt to create three sinkholes that deepened and joined to create Walden Pond. A fourth shallow sinkhole, Wyman Meadow, toggles back and forth between being part of the lake and being a fertile marsh.

The nineteenth century spans only the tiniest sliver of time since the glaciers disappeared. Nevertheless, within that century, this beautiful but ordinary lake achieved worldwide fame. In the 1820s, Thoreau began visiting Walden Pond with his family. In the 1830s, Ralph Waldo Emerson and his transcendentalists began visiting Thoreau's Cove while musing about the nature of human nature. The arrival of the railroad at Sandbank Cove brought new opportunities and challenges. One of those opportunities was creating a new pedestrian pathway, especially for a young man named Henry David Thoreau, who walked the tracks so often that he was mistaken as a railroad employee.

In 1845 Henry built himself a Simple House in the woods so he could immerse himself into nature; find the right balance between society and solitude; enjoy Waterfront activities; perform an agricultural experiment in his Bean Field; and write manuscripts that would later be published and globally appreciated. The locations of the six stops comprising "Thoreau's World" can all be seen from across the pond at the Observatory. During the winter of 1846–1847, he watched "a hundred" Irish immigrants arrive by railroad to transform Ice Fort Cove into an industrial-scale quarry. Within a decade, that same railroad was precipitating massive woodcutting of the Walden perimeter and bringing urban residents to the Concord countryside for lake recreation.

The twentieth century brought equally great changes. Thoreau's rise to literary fame was accelerated by publication of his *Journal* in

1906. The House Site became an increasingly popular mecca for literary pilgrims. With the spread of personal automobiles, the Eastern Shore became wildly popular for cooling off on hot summer days. Creation of Walden Pond State Reservation in 1922 introduced the paradox of requiring the park to be two things at once: a place of waterfront recreation *and* of historic conservation. Changes to the water quality began to show up in the 1930s. Through the late 1950s, the Eastern Shore was dramatically reshaped for recreation as trails were cut, bluffs excavated, beaches built, stone imported, concrete poured, and fish poisoned. At Deep Cove, a futile attempt to drain the pond reveals how managers misunderstood the pond's hydrology. Since the 1980s, priority has been given to conserving Walden Pond as a cultural icon for thinking environmentally, valuing self-reliance, seeking spiritual richness through voluntary simplicity, and cherishing quiet reflection in nature. The importance of Walden and *Walden* increase each year.

Our best perspective on the twenty-first century emerged from our final stop, Panorama. From this widest view over the lake, we compared and contrasted the *then* of Thoreau's world with the *now* of our present modernity. The woodland is richer. The water quality is poorer. The climate is warmer. The visitor profile has changed. People are coming in greater numbers from all over the world.

But the biggest change of all involves the fame of Thoreau's *Walden*. It went from being a book read by just a few literary specialists in English to one being read by untold millions in dozens of world languages. In the process, an ordinary pond became an extraordinary place.

One important thing remains unchanged. Walden Pond endures as a beautiful, four-season source of inspiration for anyone who follows in the footsteps of Henry David Thoreau.

# ACKNOWLEDGMENTS

My greatest debts are to those who published five works that became indispensable resources informing this guide. Chief among them is the architectural historian W. Barksdale Maynard for his masterful *Walden Pond: A History* (2004). Nearly as important were the highly technical scientific Water-Resources Investigation Reports (2001) by Paul J. Friesz and John A. Colman on the *Hydrology and Trophic Ecology* and the *Geohydrology and Limnology* of Walden Pond. The Massachusetts Department of Conservation and Recreation's anonymous *Resource Management Plan: Walden Planning* was a trove of useful information on a variety of topics, especially the ecology and visitation patterns. Jeffrey Cramer's "Fully Annotated Edition" of Thoreau's *Walden* (2004) has long enriched my reading of this challenging work. The fifth source was my own *Walden's Shore* (2014). My debt here is to editor John Kulka, the staff at Harvard University Press, and to everyone acknowledged in that team project. Five photos from this guide were first published there.

Special thanks go to Kristine Hoy Thorson, who suggested that I write this guide and collaborated with me from beginning to end. The manuscript was greatly improved by her reading of multiple drafts. Lisa White, my acquisition editor at Houghton Mifflin Harcourt, helped shape the direction and audience for the book. Production editor Beth Burleigh Fuller literally made it happen. Eugenie Delaney, designer/compositor, combined this project's many elements into a beautiful book. Emily Snyder, editorial assistant, was part of the team at every step. Lisa Adams, my agent at the Garamond Agency, was consistently supportive. The board and staff of the Walden Woods Project were my collaborators, especially Kathi Anderson, Matt Burne, Jeffrey Cramer, and Whitney Retallic. Cramer repeatedly provided encouragement, expert advice, and archival help. Richard Smith helped review and fact-check an early version of the manuscript. Conversations with Robert Gross helped clarify the local history. The Thoreau Society waived permission fees for use of their images. Staff at the Massachusetts Department of Conservation and Recreation, notably Jennifer Ingram, David Kimball, and Jacqui Luft, helped enthusiastically whenever I asked. Leslie Perrin Wilson and Conni Manoli provided archival help at the Concord Free Public Library. Barksdale Maynard willingly shared his original source notes with me during our research correspondence. My geoscience colleague, Will Ouimet, sourced the LiDAR imagery.

My expertise with *Walden* and Thoreau emerged while teaching an honors course in American Studies at the University of Connecticut variously with Professors Robert A. Gross, Wayne Franklin, Christopher Clark, Janet Pritchard, Sydney Landon-Plum, and Matthew MacKenzie. I'm especially grateful to our countless students whose tough questions and clever insights prompted my learning. The responsibility for errors, however, is mine alone.

Michael Frederick, Jayne Gordon, and Sarah Luria unknowingly precipitated the writing of this guide. Separately, each invited me to guide members of their respective national organizations around Walden Pond to help celebrate Thoreau's bicentennial birthday. When preparing for these tours, my two-page handout unexpectedly mushroomed into this book project.

Finally, I thank countless unnamed others who've toured the pond with me during the last three decades.

# NOTES

## General

Notes are referenced to text using key words (in italics) from a direct quote, the central idea, or the opening words of a sentence or paragraph, as warranted. The first reference to a source uses the full citation. Subsequent references to the same source use abbreviated titles.

Five key sources were so important they are highlighted here as abbreviated titles followed by the full citation:

**Friesz and Colman, *Hydrology.*** Paul J. Friesz and John A. Colman, *Geohydrology and Limnology of Walden Pond, Concord, Massachusetts,* U.S. Geological Survey Water-Resources Investigations Report 01-4137 (Washington, DC: U.S. Geological Survey, 2001). See also, by the same authors, *Hydrology and Trophic Ecology of Walden Pond, Concord, Massachusetts* (USGS WRI Report 01-4153, 2001).

**M-DCR, *Walden Planning.*** Massachusetts Department of Conservation and Recreation, *Resource Management Plan: Walden Planning* (Boston, MA: DCR, 2013).

**Maynard, *History.*** W. Barksdale Maynard, *Walden Pond: A History* (New York: Oxford University Press, 2004).

**Thoreau, *Walden.*** Henry David Thoreau, *Walden: A Fully Annotated Edition,* edited by Jeffrey S. Cramer (New Haven, CT: Yale University Press, 2004).

**Thorson, *Walden's Shore*.** Robert M. Thorson, *Walden's Shore: Henry David Thoreau and Nineteenth-Century Science* (Cambridge, MA: Harvard University Press, 2014).

This Guide, being written for general readers, refers back to these five principal sources for unspecified scholarly documentation of unsourced ideas, commonly used phrases, and short quotes. Information not present in these five sources is cited separately and specifically.

## Maps

The perimeter outline for all maps was traced from the official 2017 Trail Map of Walden Pond State Reservation, courtesy of David Kimball. The digital elevation model (DEM) is derived from LiDAR data (Light Detection and Ranging) provided by the Massachusetts Office of Geographic Information within the Massachusetts Executive Office for Administration and Finance.

## Timelines

Timelines for "*Walden,* the Author" and "*Walden,* the Book" follow Jeffrey S. Cramer's "Chronology" in *Henry David Thoreau in Context,* edited by James S. Finley (New York: Cambridge University Press, 2017), xxvi–xxxvii. The timelines for "Walden, the Place" and "Walden, the Landform" follow Maynard, *History,* and Thorson, *Walden's Shore,* respectively.

## Preface

*guiding all sorts of groups:* My site expertise developed from teaching "Honors: Walden and the American Landscape" (American Studies 1700) at the University of Connecticut, and conducting tours for the National Endowment for the Humanities, the Geological Society of America, the Thoreau Society, the Association of American Geographers, Channing Memorial Church in Newport, Rhode Island, and private groups.

*My take-home message:* Thorson, *Walden's Shore,* a peer-reviewed scholarly work of literary criticism, develops these ideas at length.

*a copiously illustrated guide:* This book is the first general guide to Walden Pond. In 2012, I published a chapter, "The Geology of Walden Pond," in *Guidebook for Field Trips in Connecticut and Massachusetts,* Guidebook Number 9, edited by Margaret A. Thomas (Hartford, CT: State Geological and Natural History Survey of Connecticut, 2012).

*By "park," I mean:* M-DCR, *Walden Planning* is a 142-page report summarizing legal and management issues. Refer also to their 2017 Trail Map.

*a school of philosophy:* Maynard, *History, 33–34.*

*"earth's eye":* This is the first of hundreds of uncited quotes from Thoreau's *Walden,* many of which are well known; other, less familiar Thoreau quotes are sourced separately.

*exact GPS coordinates:* Obtained via Google Earth and cross-referenced to the official 2017 DCR Trail Map of the Walden Pond State Reservation (WPSR). Elevations are approximate.

## Preparation

### Fame

*"extinct gravel-pit":* Maynard, *History,* 124. Gravel pits are mapped by Carl Koteff, *Surficial Geology of the Concord Quadrangle, Massachusetts*, U.S. Geological Survey Map GQ-331, 1964, scale 1:24,000.

*kettle lakes and ponds that speckle:* Robert M. Thorson's *Beyond Walden: The Hidden History of America's Kettle Lakes and Ponds* (New York: Bloomsbury, 2009) puts Walden Pond in a national perspective.

*The short answer is:* For 2017 essays on Thoreau's literary reputation and his role in popular culture, political history, and environmentalism, consult Finley, *Context,* especially Chapter 29, "The Evolution of Thoreau's Reputation," by Richard J. Schneider, 303–312.

*Prior to Thoreau's 1862 death:* Edward Abbey, "Down the River with Henry Thoreau" in *Down the River* (New York: Penguin/Plume Books, 1991), 20.

*"hyper-canonical status":* Robert Sattelmeyer, "Depopulation, Deforestation, and the Actual Walden Pond," *Thoreau's Sense of Place,* edited by Richard J. Schneider (Iowa City: University of Iowa Press, 2000), 235–243.

*"scripture":* Stanley Cavell, *The Senses of Walden* (New York: Viking, 1972), 16.

*"[Thoreau] was talking to Mr. Alcott":* Thoreau, *Fully Annotated Edition,* 148. This account may be exaggerated.

*This book introduces:* Annotations for the sidebar quotes provide general ecological descriptions derived from a variety of sources, such as nature guides, scholarly taxonomic websites, and Thoreau's own interpretations. Some of his taxonomic assignments are questionable. My source for *Walden* quotes is Henry D. Thoreau, *Walden* and *On the Duty of Civil Disobedience* (Project Gutenberg, 2011, http://www.gutenberg.org/files/205/205.txt), which closely parallels Thoreau, *Fully Annotated,* except for in-word dashes.

*Thoreau was never the hermit:* Thoreau's social biography has recently been updated by Laura Dassow Walls, *Henry David Thoreau: A Life* (Chicago: University of Chicago Press, 2017).

*"beautiful, vigorous, supple prose":* Joyce Carol Oates, "Introduction," in *Walden: The Writings of Henry D. Thoreau,* edited by J. Lyndon Shanley (Princeton: Princeton University Press, 1989), xii.

*book of his place:* The duality of book and place (from Cavell, *The Senses of Walden*), gave structure to Thorson, *Walden's Shore* and is a fundamental organizing principle of this Guide.

Preview

The maps will greatly help in reading this section.

*modeling himself after the young Charles Darwin:* Links to Darwin in Thorson, *Walden's Shore,* 102, 119–123, and 129–131. Prior to this transition, Alexander von Humboldt (1769–1859) had been an inspiration to both Darwin and Thoreau.

*"Enviable!":* Richard Ruland (editor), *Twentieth Century Interpretations of* Walden (Englewood Cliffs, NJ: Prentice Hall, 1968), 8.

*points submerged:* The bathymetry from 55–65 feet deep on the official Trail Map resembles that from Thoreau's Cove from 5–15 feet deep. The original tip of Sandbank Cove was pointed.

### People

Three sources—Maynard's *History,* M-DCR's *Walden Planning,* and Walls, *Henry David Thoreau: A Life*—provide a vast amount of current information on the subject.

*maximum of 1,000 people:* This is a loose estimate based on closure when the parking lots are full.

### Questions

*three basic questions:* Interpretive goals associated with the new Visitor Center are in M-DCR, *Walden Planning,* 52–53. I shortened the first question from "What do you think makes ..."

### Using This Guide

*Sidebars highlight information:* Some sidebars are linked to *Walden* using Thoreau's *Journal,* available at http://thoreau.library. ucsb.edu/writings_journals.html.

## The Tour
### Northeast: Our World
### 1: Simple House

*he called it a house:* In *Walden,* and by my count, Thoreau used the word *house* about 100 times for general description and identification and 63 times specifically as *my house.* In contrast, he used the words *cabin* and *hut* on two occasions each for literary effect.

*"discontent":* This was Thoreau's choice of words in *Walden* to describe the winter.

*"ground truth" measurements:* Roland Wells Robbins, *Discovery at Walden* (Concord, MA: Thoreau Society, 1999; reprinted from 1947).

*details of the original:* Restoration architect John Vose Goff, speaking at the 2017 Annual Gathering of the Thoreau Society (July 11–16), gave evidence that Thoreau's house was built with a center kingpost, which required an offset door. See meeting abstract.

*lawyer's office:* Maynard, *History,* 72.

*"wooden inkstand":* William Ellery Channing, *Thoreau: The Poet-Naturalist,* edited by F. B. Sanborn (Boston: Charles E. Goodspeed, 1902), 230.

*"My furniture, part of which":* Much of this is in the Concord Museum. A catalog of items is in David F. Wood, *An Observant Eye: The Thoreau Collection at the Concord Museum* (Concord, MA: The Concord Museum, 2006).

*called the "Walden Delta":* J. Walter Goldthwait, "The Sand Plains of Glacial Lake Sudbury," *Bulletin of the Museum of Comparative Zoology at Harvard College* 42 (1905).

*Thoreau word-mapped the ancient delta plain:* See Thorson, *Walden's Shore,* 39, 124–127.

### 2: Terrace Edge

*"chaise with his grandmother":* Franklin B. Sanborn, *Henry D. Thoreau* (Boston: Houghton Mifflin, 1882), 11. See also Walls, *A Life,* 37.

*This "Wyman Lot":* As used here, this is the 11 acres Emerson bought at auction and the 3 to 4 additional acres from Heartwell Bigelow, as shown by Thoreau's survey 31a held in Special Collections, Concord Free Public Library. Maynard, *History, 60–61.* Robert A. Gross shared unpublished information about the 11-acre sale.

*Henry's ancient river (sidebar):* Thorson, *Walden's Shore,* 133–135.

*Heywood "hired workmen":* Maynard, *History,* 105.

*"water, water, everywhere":* Allusion to Samuel Taylor Coleridge's *Rime of the Ancient Mariner.*

*But how did the stagnant ice:* The glacial geology reported in Thorson, *Walden's Shore,* is based on mapping by Carl Koteff, *Surficial Geology of the Concord Quadrangle,* and chronology by Jack Ridge, North American Glacial Varve Project, Tufts University, http://eos.tufts.edu/varves/NEVC/nevcdeglac.asp, accessed June 2017. The dearth of gravel between Walden's three main basins (Freisz and Colman, *Geohydrology,* 2001, Figure 2) indicates that the residual ice masses were only shallowly buried at the center, if at all.

*Thoreau knew this:* Thorson, *Walden's Shore,* 82–83, citing Thoreau's *Journal* for February 3, 1852.

*Walden Pond is a kettle:* The explicit definition of kettles, the history of terminology, and the distinction between lakes and ponds is elaborated in Thorson*, Beyond Walden,* 1–2, 115–116, and 53–54. The definitive *Glossary of Geology* (American Geological Institute) is clear on this point.

### 3: Eastern Shore

*This number staggers belief:* Maynard, *History,* 238.

*From these measurements:* Thoreau's original 1846 survey is available in the "Thoreau's Survey" online exhibit of the Special Collections of the Concord Free Public Library, item 133a, https://concordlibrary.org/special-collections/thoreau-surveys/133a. For narratives of the survey see Patrick Chura, *Thoreau the Land Surveyor* (Gainesville, FL: University Press of Florida, 2010), 22–44, and Thorson, *Walden's Shore,* 262–270.

*a narrow "pebbly beach":* Maynard, *History*, 208. The Gleason quote is from his photo caption.

*The popularity of this beach as a "swimming place":* The story is detailed in multiple chapters by M-DCR, *Walden Planning,* and by Maynard, *History.*

*"blacktop parking":* Walter Harding, "Recollections of the Early Days of the Thoreau Society," in Edmund Schofield and Robert C. Baron, eds., *Thoreau's World and Ours: A Natural Legacy* (Golden, CO: North American Press, 1993), xvi.

*Luckily, its toxic leachate:* Freisz and Colman, *Hydrology,* show the landfill boundary only 300 feet north of the groundwater divide.

*an injunction to stop the destruction:* Cindy Hill Coutre, "Walden Restoration and Legal and Policy Issues," in Schofield and Baron, *Thoreau's World,* 272–280.

*"sand is added to a created beach":* M-DCR, *Walden Planning,* 49.

**4: Boulder Wall**

*On Thursday morning:* Sourced by Roland Robbins, *Discovery at Walden,* 55–56, to page 8 of the July 27, 1878, issue of the obscure spiritualist periodical *Banner of Light.*

*"Stone walls hold time":* Robert M. Thorson, *Stone by Stone* (New York: Walker & Co., 2003), 229.

*"made out of Chaos and Old Night":* Henry D. Thoreau, *The Maine Woods* (Boston: Houghton Mifflin, 1893, Riverside Edition), 95.

*the variety of rock types:* Recent review by Thorson, *Walden's Shore,* 34–51, adapted from mapping by E-an Zen et al., *Bedrock Geologic Map of Massachusetts* (U.S. Geological Survey National Geologic Data Base, 1983), https://ngmdb.usgs.gov/Prodesc/proddesc_16357.htm, accessed June 2017.

*a century of stone-throwing:* Sample calculations show that the loss of stones by human action is plausible. For a perimeter of 1.6 miles (107,712 inches) there would be 21,542 stones averaging 5 inches across. During a span of 170 years, a one-stone perimeter could be cleared by only 119 people throwing one stone per year.

## Northwest: Thoreau's World

### 5: Bare Peak

*"clear and deep green well":* For the optics, see Robert Wetzel, *Limnology, Lake and River Ecosystems, 3rd ed.* (New York: Academic Press, 2001), 64. Hawthorne quote cited in Maynard, *History,* 50.

*Now let's sweep our eyes:* What Thoreau called Wooded Peak is now called Heywood Peak.

*We now turn around:* The details of the formation of Walden's western basin are presented in Figure 19 of Thorson, *Walden's Shore,* 145–148. The total height is from the bedrock upward to the projected delta plain. See Freisz and Colman, *Hydrology, Figure 2.*

### 6: Thoreau's Cove

*slaughterhouse for beef:* Maynard, *History,* 217–218.

*so-called* Wyman Road: Thoreau mapped the road in 1857 (survey 31a, Concord Free Public Library, Special Collections, Thoreau's Surveys). Edward Emerson sketched this road in 1920, as reproduced by Thoreau, *Fully Annotated,* 153.

*"In proportion as":* Thoreau's Cove is consistently named by every scholar, though it apparently had no name prior to Thoreau's arrival. W. Barksdale Maynard, "The Cove Names of Walden—Corrected," *Thoreau Society Bulletin* 239 (Spring 2002), unpaginated online.

*The water was plenty warm:* The hydrology, limnology, and aqueous chemistry of Walden Pond are elegantly reported by Friesz and Colman, *Hydrology.*

*Ramsey was a literary pilgrim:* Maynard, *History,* 224.

### 7: Wyman Meadow

*"wind whispering among the reeds":* Wyman Meadow is a fairly windless place and reeds (rushes) are present, but limited. Thoreau was likely referring to either Flint's Pond or Fairhaven Pond, where reeds are abundant and the wind more constant.

*"The pond rises and falls"*: Thorson, *Walden's Shore,* 194–197 details this phenomenon.

*A recent mathematical:* John Nevison, "How Walden Works: Four Models of the Hydrology of Walden Pond," in press for *The Concord Saunterer* 25 (2017).

*Ecologists classify Wyman Meadow:* Edmund Schofield, "The Ecology of Walden Woods," in Schofield and Baron, *Thoreau's World,* 155–171; and M-DCR, *Walden Planning*, plants in Appendix F, 78–84, and animals in Appendixes H–L, 90–97.

## 8: House Site

*"Mecca" was the word:* Walter Harding, "Recollections of the Early Days of the Thoreau Society," in Schofield and Baron, *Thoreau's World,* xiii–xix.

*Thoreau could have built:* Logical conjecture is an improvement over not asking the questions.

*doesn't mention a water view:* His view was a function of window size and construction, glass quality, focal distance, focal height, topography, and vegetation. Based on careful survey, when at his desk, Thoreau could see only 6 degrees of arc (about 95 feet) over distant (1300–1400 feet) Ice Fort Cove, most of which was blocked by trees.

*invited by the lady of the house:* Walls, *A Life,* 231. Thoreau left Walden a month before Waldo Emerson left for Europe, suggesting he was eager to move.

*Zilpah White, a freed slave:* The history of this poor community of freed slaves, drunks, and squatters is told by Elise Lemire, *Black Walden: Slavery and Its Aftermath in Concord, Massachusetts* (Philadelphia: University of Pennsylvania Press, 2009).

*When they reached the spot:* Maynard, *History,* 173.

*"Using my hatchet for a shovel":* Maynard, *History,* 232.

*"rude stones" of the cairn:* Maynard, *History,* 172.

*"ugly little heap":* E. B. White, "Walden" (written June 1939), *One Man's Meat* (Gardiner, ME: Tilbury House, 1997), 69.

*These cut-stone posts:* Their history is reported by Robbins, *Discovery at Walden,* 42–46. The legal issues involved in Walden Pond management are discussed by attorney Cindy Hill Couture, "Walden Restoration: Legal and Policy Issues," in Schofield and Baron, *Thoreau's World,* 199–211.

### 9: Bean Field

*the Bean Field soil is officially mapped:* More specifically, Unit 255B "Windsor loamy sand, 3 to 8 percent slopes" based on the U.S. Natural Resource Conservation Survey's Soil Survey.

*"But why should I":* Robert A. Gross, "The Great Bean Field Hoax," *The Virginia Quarterly Review* 61, No. 3 (1985) puts Thoreau's farming exercise in its social-economic context; http://www.vqronline.org/ essay/great-bean-field-hoax-thoreau-and-agricultural-reformers, accessed September 2017.

### 10: Waterfront

*In late autumn:* The story of Stuart Hotham is told by Maynard, *History,* 165–168.

*twelve lines raying out:* Concord Free Public Library, Online Exhibit, Thoreau's Surveys, 133a.

*Whereas Henry Thoreau lived:* Ibid.

*In* Walden's *"Conclusion":* Sketch of Thoreau's Waterfront in Abigail May Alcott, *Concord Sketches* (Boston: Fields, Osgood & Co., 1869).

*Astonishingly, old-school scholar:* Raymond Adams was elected president again and again until 1955. The next four presidents, Herbert F. West, Howard Zahniser, Edwin Way Teale, and Lyndon Shanley, all took their highest degrees in English. More recently, scholar Jeffrey Cramer, *The Quotable Thoreau* (Princeton, NJ: Princeton University Press, 2011), xxx–xxxiii, also concludes that the actual experience of the physical pond "mattered little," or was "a minor part" of the end result.

*most notably Charles Darwin's:* Thorson, *Walden's Shore,* 121–123 and 131–135, documents the Darwin connection.

*The deepest and most tranquil part:* Marjorie Green Winkler, "Changes at Walden Pond During the Last 600 Years," in Schofield and Baron, *Thoreau's World,* 199–211.

*By 1939 the lake:* Friesz and Colman, *Hydrology.*

*golden brown algae:* Curt Stager et al., "A 1500-year Record of Environmental Change from Walden Pond, MA," *Geological Society of America Abstracts with Programs* 48: 2 (2016).

## Southwest: Walden's Star

### 11: Ice Fort Cove

*Fun Fact: . . . Spiritualism:* Maynard, *History,* 171.

*The western window (sidebar):* Based on an instrumentally surveyed reconstruction at the house footprint with the optical center of a transit 45 inches above the ground, 27 inches back from the chain, and for a centered window 30.5 inches wide.

*ice-cutting operation (sidebar):* much of Ice Fort Cove is invisible from Thoreau's house, being hidden behind the intervening headland. He could see the cutting, not the ice "fort."

*ladies with parasols:* Maynard, *History,* 116.

*By the time the Lake Walden:* George B. Bartlett, *Concord: Historic, Literary, and Picturesque* (Boston: Lothrop Publishing, 1895).

### 12: Sandbank Cove

*it was "a torment":* Hawthorne, *American Notebooks,* Claude M. Simpson, editor (Columbus, OH: Ohio State University Press, 1992), 394–396.

*The metaphorical* Machine: Leo Marx, *The Machine in the Garden:*

*Technology and the Pastoral Ideal in America* (New York: Oxford University Press, 1964).

*Pond historian Barksdale:* Maynard, "Cove Names."

*Percival Meigs:* Ibid.

*In 1928, this southwestern:* M-DCR, *Walden Planning,* Appendix E, 78.

### 13: Deep Cove

*In* Walden, *Thoreau writes:* Maynard, "Cove Names."

*A fascinating but failed effort:* Maynard, *History,* 255.

*Thoreau emphasized to his readers:* Friesz and Colman, *Hydrology.*

### 14: Observatory

*"rule of the two diameters":* Thoreau used the geometric holism of Walden Pond as the most important metaphor for the spiritual holism he was seeking. See Thorson, *Walden's Shore,* 270, and Walls, *A Life,* 207.

*Finally, the center of the lake:* Thorson, *Walden's Shore,* 171–198, provides a detailed technical overview of the Walden system.

*New England is widely known:* Thoreau's *Walden* follows a seasonal structure. During his final years, he became very interested in seasonal patterns, a subject now called *phenology.*

### Southeast: Re-entry
### 15: Panorama

*There may be two:* The lake appears largest from this point because the maximum widths of both basins are in sight.

*Panorama is also the best:* M-DCR, *Walden Planning,* i.

*This we learned in 2013:* M-DCR, *Walden Planning,* Visitor Survey, Appendix Q, 102–116. Data is from Table 1.6.1 on page 107. Data based on 131 respondents. Percentages exceed 100 because the survey allowed more than one answer.

Ice on Walden Pond breaks up earlier now than during Thoreau's time.

*The overall terrestrial ecology:* Richard Primack, *Walden Warming: Climate Change Comes to Walden Woods* (Chicago: University of Chicago Press, 2014).

*Thoreau was rightly claimed as:* Thorson, *Walden's Shore,* 14, cites: *prophet,* Bill McKibben, "Introduction," *Walden* (Boston: Beacon Press, 2004); *founding father,* Laura Walls, "Believing in Nature," in Schneider, *Thoreau's Sense of Place,* 17; *patron saint,* Lawrence Buell, *The Environmental Imagination* (Cambridge, MA: Harvard University Press, 1995), 115.

Looking Back

*Thoreau told this story:* Thorson, *Walden's Shore,* 308.

# ORGANIZATIONS

*A short, alphabetical list of organizations most directly linked to Walden Pond.*

**Concord Free Public Library (Special Collections).** The library's Special Collections have the most comprehensive archive of primary historic documents related to Walden Pond and Henry Thoreau. Founded in 1873.

    129 Main Street
    Concord, MA 01742
    (978) 318-3345
    www.concordlibrary.org/special-collections

**Concord Museum.** The most nationally significant collection of material objects (other than documents) owned or related to Thoreau. Founded in 1886.

    53 Cambridge Turnpike
    Concord, MA 01742
    www.concordmuseum.org

**Friends of Walden Pond.** The official advocacy and fundraising component of the Walden Woods Project, as designated by the Commonwealth of Massachusetts. Founded before 2001, when it became part of the Thoreau Society, prior to its transfer to the Walden Woods Project.

44 Baker Farm Road
Lincoln, MA 01773-3004
Contact is through the website: www.walden.org/what-we-do/
friends-of-walden-pond

**Thoreau Farm Trust.** A nonprofit organization committed to preservation of Thoreau's birthplace on Virginia Road in Concord, Massachusetts. Founded in 1995.
341 Virginia Road
Concord, MA 01742
info@thoreaufarm.org
www.thoreaufarm.org

**Thoreau Institute.** (Officially the Walden Woods Project's Thoreau Institute.) The physical, administrative, and scholarly home of the Walden Woods Project. The institute's offices, library archive, and conservation facilities make it a center for scholarly research, public education, and conservation. Founded in 1998.
44 Baker Farm Road
Lincoln, MA 01773-3004
(781) 259-4700
www.walden.org/property/the-thoreau-institute

**Thoreau Society.** The oldest and largest U.S. organization devoted to an author. The Thoreau Society publishes *The Concord Saunterer* and the *Thoreau Society Bulletin* and holds an annual July gathering. Housed in the restored birth home of Thoreau. Founded in 1941.
341 Virginia Road
Concord, MA 01742
(978) 369-5310
www.thoreausociety.org

**Walden Pond State Reservation (WPSR).** For all practical purposes, this is an internationally significant state park containing Walden Pond and the surrounding land. The WPSR is managed by the Massachusetts Department of Conservation and Recreation. Founded in 1922.

915 Walden Street
Concord, MA 01742
(978) 369-3254
walden.pond@state.ma.us
www.mass.gov/eea/agencies/dcr/massparks/region-north/walden-pond-state-reservation.html

**Walden Woods Project (WWP).** A nonprofit organization founded to preserve the land, literature, and legacy of Henry David Thoreau. WWP is the umbrella organization for the Thoreau Institute at Walden Woods and the Friends of Walden Pond. Founded in 1990.

44 Baker Farm Road
Lincoln, MA 01773-3004
(781) 259-4700
www.walden.org

# FURTHER READINGS

*An annotated select list of resources for the reader to consult for further information, alphabetized by topic.*

**Biography.** *Henry David Thoreau: A Life,* by Laura Dassow Walls (Chicago: University of Chicago Press, 2017). The definitive new biography of Henry David Thoreau published on the occasion of Thoreau's bicentennial.

**Climate.** *Walden Warming: Climate Change Comes to Walden Woods,* by Richard Primack (Chicago: University of Chicago Press, 2014). A principle source for ecological climate change issues at Walden Pond. A very readable gathering of the relevant literature.

**Context.** *Henry David Thoreau in Context,* edited by James S. Finley (New York: Cambridge University Press, 2017). A reference collection of thirty-four topical essays by experts that put Thoreau and *Walden* into context. See also *Thoreau at 200: Essays and Reassessments,* edited by Kevin P. Van Anglen and Kristen Case (Cambridge: Cambridge University Press, 2016).

**History.** *Walden Pond: A History,* by W. Barksdale Maynard (New York: Oxford University Press, 2004). The definitive narrative history of Walden Pond. Many of the uncited historic facts in this guidebook were drawn from this secondary source, which cites the primary sources.

**Lake Walden.** *Hydrology and Trophic Ecology of Walden Pond, Concord, Massachusetts,* U.S. Geological Survey Water-Resources Investigations Report 01-4153, by Paul J. Friesz and John A. Colman (Washington, DC: U.S. Geological Survey, 2001). My principal source for the hydrology and aquatic ecology of the pond. An excellent one-stop document for the physical attributes of the pond and how it works.

**Landscape.** *Walden's Shore: Henry David Thoreau and Nineteenth-Century Science,* by Robert M. Thorson (Cambridge, MA: Harvard University Press, 2014). The physical environment of Walden Pond, its geological creation story, and the historic scientific context of *Walden.* This book details Thoreau's understanding of Walden Pond and how that influenced *Walden.*

**Management and Terrestrial Ecology.** *Walden Planning Resource Management Plan,* by the Massachusetts Department of Conservation and Recreation (Boston, MA: DCR, 2013). This document provides an overview of park visitation, regulatory issues, and an inventory of all natural resources.

**Material Culture.** *An Observant Eye: The Thoreau Collection at the Concord Museum,* by David F. Wood (Concord, MA: Concord Museum, 2006). The best print source for information about Thoreau's material possessions, beautifully described.

**Photography.** *Historic: "Earth's Eye": An Online Exhibition of Walden Pond Images,* edited by Leslie Perrin Wilson (Concord, MA: Concord Free Public Library, 2004). An online exhibit of 51 historic photographs from the special collections, with an introduction by W. Barksdale Maynard. ***Modern:*** *Thoreau's Walden: A Journey in Photographs,* by Scot Miller (Boston, MA: Houghton Mifflin, 2004). The full text of *Walden* highlighted by large-format color photographs.

**Walden:** *Walden: A Fully Annotated Edition,* edited by Jeffrey S. Cramer (New Haven, CT: Yale University Press, 2004). The best edition for the novice reader of *Walden.* The extensive annotations enhance understanding of the text. My students recommend this text.

**Wildlife:** ***General:*** *National Audubon Society Field Guide to New England,* compiled by Peter Alden and others (New York: Alfred Knopf, 1998), provides a comprehensive guide for identifying the plants and animals of Walden Woods. ***Specific:*** *Thoreau's Animals,* edited by Geoff Wisner (New Haven, CT: Yale University Press, 2017).

**Woodlands.** *Thoreau and the Language of Trees,* by Richard Higgins (Oakland, CA: University of California Press, 2017). A soulful resource to Thoreau's trees. See also *Reading the Forested Landscape: A Natural History of New England,* by Tom Wessels (Woodstock, VT: Countryman Press, 1999), for interpreting forest history.

Tip of Thoreau's Cove in late summer shows lush growth of aquatic plants in shallow water and weedy, eroded shore. This view is very near the bridge of Stop 7, Wyman Meadow.

# INDEX

Notes: Entries in **bold** indicate photos/illustrations. Entries in sidebars are referenced by "sb."

*Acer rubrum. See* Maple, red

*Acer saccharum. See* Maple, sugar

Adams, Mary Newbury, 24, 128

Adams, Raymond: granite posts, 130; "old school," 151, 229; Thoreau Society, 119

Alcott, Abigail May Neiricker: 153sb; sketch, **144**; sketch interpretation, 148; visitor, 128

Alcott, Bronson: friend, 15, 35, 120; house guest, 121; 194sb; Thoreau memorial, 128, 131; visitor, xx, 11–12

Alder, speckled (*Alnus incana ssp. rugosa*), 66sb

Allegories, Thoreau's: ant war, 69sb; loon, 89sb; Mother Nature, 214; old settler, 214; origin of pond, 54–55; stony shore, 55

*Alnus incana ssp. rugosa. See* Alder, speckled

*Amble, the Emerson-Thoreau,* 151

*Ameiurus nebulosus. See* Pout, horned

Amusement park. *See* Walden Lake Grove Excursion Park

Ancient delta plain: definition, 44; analogs of, **43**, **71**; occurrences, 44, 51, 59, 87, 135, 141, 168, 169, **173**; Thoreau's interpretation, 45

Angle of repose: Bare Peak, **86**, 90, 91

Animals in sidebars (at stops): ants (Stop 3), 69sb; whirlygig beetles (Stop 11), 162sb; red fox (Stop 12), 172sb; Canada geese (Stop 10), 147sb; snowshoe hare (Stop 8), 118sb; human (Stop 15), 203sb; common loon (Stop 5), 89sb; deer mice (Stop1), 36sb; great horned owl (Stop 4), 77sb; chain pickerel (Stop 2), 50sb; yellow perch, (Stop 6), 96sb; horned pout (Stop 7, brown bullhead), 106sb; American robin (Stop 13), 180sb; red squirrel (Stop 14), 190sb; woodchuck (Stop 9), 138sb

Ant, red and black (*no species assignment*), **68**

Anthropocene, 70; *See also* Geological history

Aquifer, of Walden: exposure of, 51; properties of, 115, 187; behavior of, 52, 107, 183, 184, 195

*Index*

At a Glance summaries: Bare Peak
(Stop 5), 87; Bean Field (Stop 9),
136; Boulder Wall (Stop 4), 72;
Eastern Shore (Stop 3), 60; Deep
Cove (Stop 13), 178; definition, 28;
House Site (Stop 8), 116; Ice Fort
Cove (Stop 11), 158; Observatory
(Stop 14), 188; Panorama (Stop
15), 200; Sandbank Cove (Stop
12), 170; Simple House (Stop
1), 34; Terrace Edge (Stop 2),
46; Thoreau's Cove (Stop 6), 94;
Waterfront (Stop 10), 144; Wyman
Meadow (Stop 7), 104

Bare Peak: general, 18, 27, **91**, 94, 97,
125, 189, 214; Stop 5, **87**–93
Basin, kettle, 56–58, 62, 99. *See also*
Kettle
Beaches: Main Beach, **4**, 16, 64–**67**;
**4**, **53**, **71**, **202**–**203**; original
condition, **53**, 63–**64**; Red Cross
Beach, 66–**67**; Sandbank Cove,
**170**, 176; Waterfront, 145, **149**
Bean Field, general, 18, **27**, 111, 134,
191, 215; Stop 9, **136**–143
Bedrock: below Walden, 46, **75**, 80;
buried valley, 45, **62**; symbolism,
73
*Betula populifolia. See* Birch, gray
Blueberry, highbush (*Vaccinium
corymbosum*), **30**, 111sb
Biodiversity, 29, 110
Birch, gray (*Betula populifolia*), **41**,
40sb
Boat launch, 83, 210
Boulder from moraine, **92**
Boulder Wall: general, 17, 27, **75**, 210,
214; Stop 4, **72**–82
Brennan, Thomas B.: building
program, 24, 81sb; pumping, 182

*Branta canadensis. See* Geese,
Canada
*Bubo virginianus. See* Owl, great
horned

Cairn, memorial: disappearance of,
130; early photo, **129**; initiation
of, 24, 128–129; importance, 18;
source, 82; theft from, **28**
*Carya* sp. *See* Hickory
Cellar: Thoreau's, 18, 122, 130; other,
48, 126–127
Central Basin, 87, 199, **212**
Chain of Ponds, 20, 49sb, **62**
Channing, William Ellery, the
younger, 15, 38, 120, 128
Climate change: glacial, 53; recent,
147, 155, 208, 209
Concord, town of, 9, 13, 35, 57, 64, 66,
78, 96, 119, 159, 179, 215
Concord Free Public Library, 25,
233
Concord Museum, 25, 42, 127, 233
Coves: definition of, 95; official
names, 20, 176; stops, 95, 159, 171,
179; submerged, 19. *See also* Deep
Cove, Ice Fort Cove, Sandbank
Cove, Thoreau's Cove
Coyle (also Quoil, Quoyle), Hugh, 23,
49, 56sb

Darwin, Charles, 18, 152
Deep Cove: general, 20, **186**, **212**,
216; Stop 13, **178**–187
Department of Conservation and
Recreation (DCR, Massachusetts),
2, 25, 111
Digital Elevation Model (DEM),
**27**. *See also back right endpaper
map*
Desk, Thoreau's writing, **132**

"earth's eye," of Walden, 4, 149

Eastern Basin, 58, 125, 201, **200**, 210. *See also front endpaper maps*

Eastern Shore: general, 16, 23, **64**, **71**, 203, 210, 216; Stop 3, **60**–71

Ecosystem: Greater Walden Woods, 24, 111; Walden's Shore, 29, 110–115

Emerson family (extended): Edward, 142; Edith (Emerson Forbes), 24, 67; Lidian, 126; Raymond, 130; William, 172. *See also* Emerson, Ralph Waldo

Emerson, Ralph Waldo, 13, 15, 18, 23, 36, 42, 49, 96, 119, 120, 126, 127, 129, 146, 183sb, 215

Emerson's Cliff, 45, 111. *See also back right endpaper map*

*Esox reticulatus. See* Pickerel, chain

Fish, stocking of Walden, 114–115

Flint's Pond, 114, 152–153

Flute, Thoreau's, 98sb

Friends of Walden Pond, 25

Footprint, of house, 18, 35sb, 37, **116**, 120–121, 133

Forbes, Edith Emerson. *See* Emerson family

Fox, red (*Vulpes vulpes*), **13**, 172sb

*Gavia immer. See* Loon, common

*Gaylussacia baccata. See* Huckleberry

Geese, Canada (*Branta canadensis*), 125, **146**, 147sb

Geological history, 74–81

Glacial Lake Sudbury, 44, 93sb, 177

Glaciation: allegory, 214; cirque 186; global cooling, 208; ice sheet glaciation, 44–45; kettle formation, 53–58; modern

analogs, **43**, **55**, **71**; sediment production, 80–81, **91**–92

Gleason, Herbert W.: General, 9, 64, 145, 176; photographs by, **52**, **64**, **91**

Goldthwait, J. Walter, 44–45, 93sb

GPS (global positioning system), 5 (*see note*)

Grape, wild (*Vitus riparia*), **206**, 207sb

Groundwater: leachate, 70, 155; flow, 51–52, 107, 184–185, 196; pumping, 182–183; table, 51, 58, 62

Hammered (cut) stone, 78sb, 130–133, **135**

Harding, Walter, 118–119, 151–152

Hardscape, at Eastern Shore, 17, **60**, 63, 66, 210. *See also* Stone walls

Hare, snowshoe (*Lepus Americanus*), 118sb, **119**

Hawthorne, Nathaniel, 15, 89, 172, 177sb

Hemlock, eastern (*Tsuga canadensis*), 111, 184sb, **185**

Henley, Don, 25

Heywood, Charles L., 167, 168sb

Heywood, George, 24, 50

Hickory (*Carya sp.*), 110, 141sb

Hollow. *See* Kettle

*Homo sapiens. See* Human

Hotham, Stuart, 146–147

House, Thoreau's original: construction, 36; description, 35sb; furnishing, 40; Sophia's sketch, **8**; timbers, 122; plaster, 38–39; boards, 120; cellar, 122; orientation on lot, 123–125

House replica. *See* Simple House

House Site: general, 1, 18, 24, 26, **27**, 29, 81, **129**, **132**; Stop 8, **116**–135

Hubbard, Cyrus, 148, 148sb
Huckleberry (*Gaylussacia baccata*),
    90, 100sb
Human, woodchopper, Alek Therian
    (*Homo sapiens*), 184, 203sb
Hydrology, of Walden: stage
    variation, 106–109, **108**; water
    budget, 183–187

Ice: glacial, 53–54; harvesting, 161–
    165; winter lake, 208, **213**, **232**
Ice Fort Cove: general, 19, 61, **101**,
    **102**, 124, **161**, **164**, **167**, **186**, 215;
    Stop 11, **158**–169
Invasive plants, 110–112
Irish immigrants, 120, 161–162, 180

Kettle: characteristics, 56;
    equivalence to basins, 58; origin
    of, 9, 53–56, **55**; terminology (hole,
    pond, lake), 57

Lake, definition, 57. *See also* Pond,
    definition of
Lake district, 3, 20, 57. *See also* Chain
    of Ponds
Lake Walden (Amusement Park).
    *See* Walden Lake Grove Excursion
    Park
Laurentide Ice Sheet, 53
*Lepus Americanus. See* Hare,
    snowshoe
LiDAR (Light Detection and
    Ranging), 168
Limnology, 155
Loon, common (*Gavia immer*), 11,
    **88**, 89sb, 193
Lower heaven, 28, 192

Maple, red (*Acer rubrum*), 166sb,
    197

Maple, sugar (*Acer saccharum*),
    174sb, 175
Maps: *sectors and themes, left
    front endpaper; stop names and
    numbers, right front endpaper;
    stops on official park map, left back
    endpaper; stops on topography,
    right back endpaper*
*Marmota monax. See* Woodchuck, or
    groundhog
Marsh, 105, 109, 109sb
Mice, deer (*Peromyscus leucopus*),
    36sb, 112
Middlesex County Commissioners,
    65–68
Moraine (ridge), 91

Nieriker, Abigail May Alcott, 144,
    147–148, 153sb
Northeast Sector (Our World), maps,
    **32–33**
Northwest Sector (Thoreau's World),
    maps, **83–85**

Oak, shrub (*Quercus ilicifolia* or
    *rubra*), 54
Oak, white (*Quercus alba*), 92sb
Observatory: general, 19, 215; Stop
    14, **188**–198
Our World (Northeast Sector). *See*
    Northeast sector
Owl, great horned (*Bubo
    virginianus*), **76**, 77sb

Panorama: general, 22, 216; Stop 15,
    **200**–211
People, in sidebars (in stops):
    Bronson Alcott (Stop 14), 194sb;
    Thomas B. Brennan (Stop 4),
    81sb; Hugh Coyle (Stop 2), 56sb;
    Ralph Waldo Emerson (Stop 13),

183sb; Edith Emerson Forbes (Stop 15), 208sb; J. Walter Goldthwait (Stop 5), 93sb; Nathaniel Hawthorne (Stop 12), 177sb; Charles L. Heywood (Stop 11), 168sb; Abigail May Alcott Nieriker (Stop 10), 153sb; Carl T. Ramsey (Stop 6), 103; Roland Robbins (Stop 1), 44sb; Sophia Thoreau (Stop 8), 134sb; Kate Tryon (Stop 3), 70sb; Hugh Whelan (Stop 9), 142sb; Tommy Wyman (Stop 7), 112sb

*Perca flavescens. See* Perch, yellow

Perch, yellow (*Perca flavescens*), 96sb, **97**, 110, 192

Peripatetic, walking, 3

*Peromyscus leucopus. See* Mice, deer

Pickerel, chain (*Esox reticulatus*), 50sb, **51**

Pilgrims, to the House Site, **24**, 72, 129–130

Pine, pitch (*Pinus rigida*), 79sb

*Pinus rigida. See* Pine, pitch

*Pinus strobus. See* Pine, white

Pine, white (*Pinus strobus*), **192**, 193sb

Places (described by Thoreau) in sidebars (at stops): ancient river (Stop 2), 49sb; astronomical allusion (Stop 14), 189sb; bay in Wyman Meadow (Stop 7), 105sb; bean field soil (Stop 9), 137sb; bedrock reality (Stop 4), 73sb; broadest view (Stop 15), 201sb; cove definition (Stop 6), 95sb; Fitchburg railroad (Stop 12), 171sb; harvesting at Ice Fort Cove (Stop 11), 160sb; house construction (Stop 1), 35sb;

isolated cove (Stop 13), 179sb; steep slope (Stop 5), 87sb; tiny beach (Stop 3), 65sb; waterfront pond-side (Stop 10), 148sb; woodsy yard (Stop 8), 117sb

Plants (trees, shrubs, vines) in sidebars (at stops): eastern hemlock (Stop 13), 184sb; gray birch (Stop 1), 40sb; hickory (Stop 9), 141sb; highbush blueberry (Stop 7), 111sb; huckleberry (Stop 6), 100sb; pitch pine (Stop 4), 79sb; red maple (Stop 11), 188sb; scrub oak (Stop 2), 54sb; smooth sumac (Stop 8), 124sb; speckled alder (Stop 3), 66sb; sugar maple (Stop 12), 174sb; white pine (Stop 14), 193sb; white oak (Stop 5), 92sb; wild grape (Stop 15), 207sb; willow, 151sb

Plaster, house, 38–39

Pollution: airborne, 115, 207; groundwater leachate, 70, 185; swimmers, 70, 185, 205

Pond definition, 57. *See also* Lake, definition of

Pond Path: construction, **vi–vii**, 85, **113**, **157**, 158, **173**; definition, 4; erosion, **16**, 69; ecology, 110

Pond-side, Thoreau's. *See* Waterfront

Pond survey, 61–62, 98–99, **101**, 123, 171, 180, **188**

Pout, horned (*Ameiurus nebulosus*), 106sb

*Quercus ilicifolia* (or *rubra*). *See* Oak, shrub

*Quercus alba. See* Oak, white

Radial symmetry, of western basin, 19, **188**, **195**

Railroad; construction, 20, 39, 120, 171; impacts, 111, 154, 157, 177sb, 180, **181**, 204; sandbank, xx; Thoreau, 12, 17, 147, 171sb, 172, 174–176, 180; MBTA, 159. *See also* Lake Walden

Ramsey, Carl T., 103sb

Realms, of Walden, 195

Re-entry (Southeast Sector), 22–23, 199

Red Cross Beach, 66, **67**

Restoration, of Walden landscape, 68–70, 69sb, 158

*Rhus glabra. See* Sumac, smooth

Robbins, Roland, 37, 44sb, 123, 131–133

Robin, American (*Turdus migratorius*), 180sb, **181**

*Salix sp. See* Willow, river

Sandbank Cove: general, 19, **173**, **186**, 215; Stop 12, **170**–177

Sandy Pond. *See* Flint's Pond

Sectors (introductions): Northeast, **32–33**; Northwest, **83–85**; Southwest, **156–157**; Southeast, **199**

"Sense of Place" texts, 28

Shantytowns, 20, 180, 209

Shaw, T. Mott, 24, 133

Shrub oak plateau. *See* Ancient delta plain

Sidebars (defined), 29–30

Simple House: general, 16, **32**, 211, 215; Stop 1, **35**–45

Sounds in sidebars (at Stops): church bells ringing (Stop 5), 90sb; cows mooing (Stop 15), 205sb; ducks quacking (Stop 14), 191sb; echoes growling (Stop 2), 53sb; flute playing (Stop 6), 98sb;

frogs croaking (Stop 7), 109sb; hymns being hummed (Stop 10), 152sb; ice cracking (Stop 3), 63sb; ice harvesting (Stop 11), 163sb; leaves whooshing (Stop 8), 121sb; raindrops pattering (Stop 1), 39sb; storm thundering (Stop 13), 182sb; stones thunking (Stop 4), 78sb; stones tinkling (Stop 9), 140sb; train whistling (Stop 12), 176sb

Sinkholes. *See* Kettle

Southeast Sector (Re-entry), *front endpapers,* **199**

Southwest Sector (Walden's Star), *endpapers,* **156–157**

Squirrel, red (*Tamiasciurus hudsonicus*), **190**, 190sb

Stone: cut, 69, 130–133, **135**; hammered, xx; natural, **156–157**; rip-rap, **83**, **102**, 174

Stone walls: boulder source, **72**, **75**, **135**, **156–157**; construction, 78sb; fieldstone source, 210–**211**, conservation, 210

Stony shore, of Walden: original, 22, 80, 81–82; loss of, 207

Sumac, smooth (*Rhus glabra*), 121sb, 122–123, 125

*Tamiasciurus hudsonicus. See* Squirrel, red

Teale, Edwin Way, 24, 202

Terrace Edge: general, 16, 23, **32**, **52**; Stop 2, **46**–59

Thoreau family, 96, 134sb

Thoreau Institute (at Walden Woods), 127

Thoreau Society, 24, 67, 118–119, 130, 133, 151–152

Thoreau, Sophia: 8, 96, 116, 134sb, 148

Thoreau's Cove: general, **3**, 18, **27**, 47, **84**, 85, **99**, **178**, **241**; Stop 6, **94**–103

Thoreau's World (Northwest Sector), 83

Timelines: author, viii; book, x; historic place, xi; landform, xiii

Transcendentalists, 3, 27, 204, 215

Tryon, Kate, 51, 63, 70sb

*Tsuga canadensis. See* Hemlock, eastern

Tudor, Frederick, 23, 162

*Turdus migratorius. See* Robin, American

Underground railroad, 13

*Vaccinium corymbosum. See* Blueberry, highbush

Van Dore, Wade, 130

Vernal pool, 109, 112

Visitor Center, 2, **3**, **6**, 15–16, 25, 47, 50, 211

*Vitus riparia. See* Grape, wild

*Vulpes vulpes. See* Fox, red

Walden Delta, 44

Walden Lake Grove Excursion Park, 57, **158**, 166, **167**–168, 168sb

Walden Paradox, 29, 202, 216

Walden Pond: named, 23, 57; created, 51–55, 58

Walden Pond attributes: independence, 20; purity, 20; renewal, 11, 22; resilience, 21; sensitivity, 21; simplicity, 20

Walden Pond State Reservation, 2, 24, 65, 202

Walden Street (Walden Road, Highway 126): early conditions, 47–48; park address, 4

Walden's Star (Southwest Sector), 156. *See also endpaper maps for shape*

Walden Woods, 24, 45, 93, 109, 111, 127, 205

Walden Woods Project, 1, 25, 127

*Walden,* drafts, xx; published, xx; manuscript, **14**

Water, lake: color of, 87–89; source of, 51–52, 182; purity of, 20; budget, 184–186

Waterfront: general, 18, **27**, **94**, 103, **149**, 191, 215; Stop 10, **144**–155

Western Basin, 19, 58, 92–93, 124–125, 145, 150, 204

Whelan, Hugh, 42, 126–127, 142sb

Willow, river (*Salix sp.*), **150**, 151sb

Windsor Soil, 136, 136sb, 141

Woodchuck, or groundhog (*Marmota monax*), 12, 122, 123, 124, 136, 138sb, **139**, 208

Wyman Lot, 49, 95, 104, 112sb, 118

Wyman Meadow: general, 18, **27**, **113**, 183, 191, 215; Stop 7, **104**–115

Wyman, Tommy, 112sb

# A MESSAGE FROM THE WALDEN WOODS PROJECT

Caring for Walden Pond and protecting Walden Woods requires constant vigilance, advocacy, and financial support. There is an important role to play for each individual who values the land that inspired Henry David Thoreau and who wants to perpetuate Thoreau's legacy to a worldwide audience.

The Walden Woods Project, a nonprofit organization founded by the recording artist Don Henley, invites you to join us in preserving the land, literature, and legacy of Henry David Thoreau.

**FRIENDS OF WALDEN POND:** The Walden Woods Project (WWP) has been designated by the Commonwealth of Massachusetts as the official "Friends of Walden Pond" group and is authorized to raise funds to help care for Walden Pond and its environs. The WWP also partners with the Massachusetts Department of Conservation and Recreation on educational programming and interpretive exhibits at the Walden Pond State Reservation Visitor Center. These initiatives tie Thoreau's ethics to today's worldwide challenges relating to the environment and social reform. One word—*Walden*—has come to represent a powerful way of thinking about urgent global issues that include addressing the challenges of climate change, safeguarding the biodiversity of life, and supporting human rights.

**LAND CONSERVATION:** Henry David Thoreau is widely known as "the father of the American conservation movement." Yet parts of his beloved Walden Woods are not protected and remain vulnerable to inappropriate development and misuse. Since 1990, the WWP has been at the forefront of the battle to preserve sites in the 2,680-acre Walden Woods, most of which lie outside the Walden Pond State Reservation and are not safeguarded. When incompatible commercial development has threatened this natural treasure, the WWP has effectively preserved the endangered lands.

**EDUCATION:** Thoreau's philosophy has never been more pertinent. His writings provide insights into some of the most urgent issues of our time. These include living on a planet of limited resources and the role of personal responsibility in today's world. The WWP's educational initiatives employ Thoreau's ideas in understanding and confronting these challenges, serving an audience of students, educators, and lifelong learners.

**SCHOLARSHIP:** The WWP provides access to a full range of materials created by Thoreau and other environmentally significant authors. The Thoreau Institute is the WWP's headquarters near Walden Pond. It includes the finest Thoreau research library in the world.

Please make a tax-deductible gift to help the Walden Woods Project care for Walden Pond, an iconic landscape known around the globe. Help us share Thoreau's legacy with the half million people who visit the Walden Pond State Reservation every year. A portion of the sales proceeds from this guide will be donated to the Friends of Walden Pond.

Kathi Anderson, Executive Director
Walden Woods Project
www.walden.org
781-259-4700
wwproject@walden.org

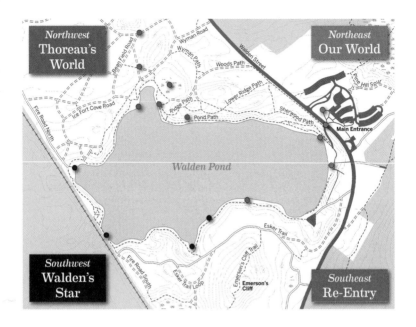

Map of Walden Pond showing our fifteen stops superimposed on the park's official 2017 Trail Map, available in the Visitor Center, courtesy of the Massachusetts Department of Conservation and Recreation. For the numbers, names, and themes of these stops, consult the two maps on the front endpapers of this guide. North is up.

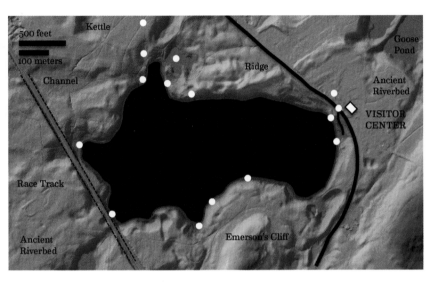

Map of Walden Pond showing the lake outline, our fifteen stops, and selected features superimposed on a high-resolution topographic map. The topography is shown as a hillside-shaded digital elevation model (DEM) created using LiDAR (Light Detection and Ranging) data, courtesy of the MassGIS office. For the numbers, names, and themes of these stops, consult the two maps on the front endpapers of this guide. Relative elevation is shown by color, with red being high and green being low. North is up. Scale is shown in upper left.